The Anti-Procrastination Mindset

The Simple Art of Finishing what you Start

(with 117 Anti-Procrastination Hacks)

Including 2
Self-Assessment
Tests

HARRY HEIJLIGERS

© 2018

SmartLeadershipHut.com/
TheAntiProcrastinationMindset

Legal Notice

Disclaimer Notice

Book Bonuses

Thank you for choosing my book! I would like to show my appreciation for the trust you gave me by giving **FREE GIFTS** for you!

If you follow this QR code with a QR reader on your smartphone, then you will arive on the website where you can collect all the accompanying book bonuses.

The following is included in the package you get for **FREE** as a Bonus to this book:

- Procrastination Signs Self-Assessment Test

- Procrastination Causes Self-Assessment Test

- Stay Focused Music Bundle

- The Eisenhower Matrix

- List of 500 Personal Values to Choose from

- Brainwaves Infographic

- Checklist for the 117 Anti-Procrastination Hacks

- Access to our Private VIP Facebook Group

Simply use the QR code on the left to download all the book bonuses!

Why I wrote this book for you

Procrastination is something we all do. I indeed do procrastinate, and, who knows, more than the average person. Procrastinating, however, is very pitiful because it stands in the way between you and achieving your goals in life. It is so much you want to accomplish in your life, so many dreams to fulfill, so many goals to reach. But to achieve all of that, most of the time, it is just a matter of doing the hard work. And that hard work you have to put in achieving your goals doesn't tolerate procrastination.

So to make myself more productive, successful and happy, I have studied myself and the field of procrastination very well so that I would be able to optimize myself continuously. I discovered that all courses and books in the area of procrastination deal with procrastination in a kind of time management like way. However, in my opinion, procrastination can't be cured on the level of behavior. So, just learning another type of to-do list, or 2-minute rule, or planning tool, is not enough. No, in my opinion, you can change your procrastination habit easily and effectively, but not by learning a new behavior or skill. Instead, if you want to change your procrastination temptation, you need to change your mindset. Mindset is the way you think, the way you view your world. Mindset is about the beliefs and values you have, about the way you look at yourself, what you say about yourself and how you say it. And it is possible to change your mindset. That's why I wrote this book for you: to teach you in simple and easy steps how to improve your mindset so that you will no longer procrastinate but instead, become a highly productive and successful goal getter. I wrote this book to teach you how you can change the way you think so that you will no longer think like a procrastinator. In this book, you will find that it is relatively easy to change your way of thinking and to change the way you view the world. Above all, I wrote this book for you so that you will become happier. With an Anti-Procrastination Mindset, you will not only be more successful and productive, but you will also be happier. But, hey, don't believe me, just check it out for yourself!

Just a warning up front: if you are looking for a quick fix or the latest time management trick, please don't buy this book! There are lots of other books which deal with that department. However, if you are looking for a permanent change in your life, this book is ideal for you! I wrote this book to help you realize a permanent change in your life by taking one small baby step at a time, all adding up to a more successful and happy You.

So, if you want to get more out of your life, and you find yourself procrastinating often, this book is ideal for you provided you are prepared to change yourself along the way in the process of becoming a goal getter. After reading this book and having implemented all the anti-procrastination hacks, you will no longer be disappointed in yourself. Heck, you will probably even not recognize yourself because you have become a totally new and optimized You! So, what are you waiting for? Let's begin!

Like one of the stonecutters you will meet in the book, I want to build Cathedrals. Well, at least metaphorically speaking. I want to have a long-lasting positive and empowering impact on countless people, even while I will probably most of them not meet in person. Because then everything I do will not be for nothing. My wish for you is that you too want to build Cathedrals, or whatever other metaphor you wish to choose for a long-lasting impact on the world around you. This book will show you Why and How. It will make you way more Successful and Happier, I promise! And above all, it will leave the Procrastinator in you, way behind you!

How to Use this Book

My First and Most Important Advice to You: Don't buy this book if you are not planning to do something with it! With that out of the way, if you still want to improve yourself, and to become more productive and to procrastinate less, then reading and acting upon this book might be the best investment you have done in your life. Think about it this way: if you manage to procrastinate 1% less every day from now on by following the Anti-Procrastination Hacks provided in this book, then every day from now on until the end of your life, you will benefit from it!

So, don't read this book passively! Read it actively! This book will provide you with a whole new mindset of doing things and of dealing with things. I have broken it down for you into 117 bite-sized Anti-Procrastination Hacks. After reading each hack, you should stop reading any further and instead start acting upon it. Engage yourself fully with the material provided by this book. My promise to you is this: with every one of the 117 Anti-Procrastination Hacks you manage to implement in your life, you will become more productive, successful and happy. Step by step. If you manage to improve yourself with only one percent each day, you will be totally unrecognizable in one year from now!

To support you in actually doing something with the material provided in this book and to implement it in your life and optimize yourself with one percent each day, I have created a special private VIP Facebook Group. In this group, I will post one Anti-Procrastination Hack every working day of the week. This will give you a continuous reminder of the material of this book. Furthermore, we can help each other keeping accountable for implementing the hacks. And, of course, if you have questions, you can also post them there. At the end of this book, you can read how you can apply for this group. It's FREE!

"Change will not come if we wait for some other person or some other time. You are the one you have been waiting for. You are the change that we seek."

- Barack Obama

Dedication

*This book is for
my lovely wife Deborah,
my daughter Chayenna,
and my son Jayden,
for their Love and Support.*

Table of Contents

Introduction

Why is it that you are not more successful than you are right now? Yes, you might be successful, right now. But let's be honest. It's only a fraction of what you are really capable of. Your current results are way under what your real potential is. So, what is it that is holding you back? What is the barrier that is keeping you from really realizing the gift and potential and capability that you have inside of you that has not been blossomed and achieved yet? Well, here is the reality: there is no silver bullet and indeed no magic pill. Instead, success is earned by doing the hard work. The truth about gaining success is this: it is mundane, it is unexciting, it is unsexy, it is laborious, it is frustrating, and sometimes it is even defeating. That's the truth about the process of earning success. So, stop looking for the quick fix for success, happiness and wealth. There isn't one. Instead, you will have to walk through a minefield of mundane, unexciting, unsexy, laborious, frustrating, and defeating hard work to get to the other side of your success journey. Success is earned one day at a time. Every day, when you wake up, you get to define and decide, whether or not that they will be a success; one decision at a time, one step at a time, one phone call at a time, one meeting at a time, one day at a time. It is not what you know which determines your success. It is only about what you do with what you know. That's why implementing the anti-procrastination hacks I will present you throughout this book is crucial. And to support you with that, I invite you to become part of our Smart Leadership Community on Facebook.

Introduction

Simply, follow the QR-code at the end of this book or, alternatively, browse to :

https://www.facebook.com/groups/slhcommunity/.

It's totally FREE! And we are supporting each other in creating better habits every day.

So, here is my goal for you: with this book I am going to provide to you a system that has the power to enable you to achieve goals you were afraid even to imagine possible. One year from now, You, Your Business, and Your Life will be totally unrecognizable.

What is the root control factor to all your outcomes in life? It's your choices! You are making hundreds of choices every day. Some of them consciously, but most choices you make subconsciously. But they are still choices. They determine whether or not you open that email. Or they determine whether or not you answer that email after you have decided to open it.

If you make better choices, your life will be more joyful and successful. So, how do you make better choices? By changing your mindset! This book teaches you how to change your mindset from being a Procrastinator into a highly successful and happy goal getter. This book is all about The Anti-Procrastination Mindset.

Throughout this book, I mention various downloadable resources I've made for you. Please, use the QR-code on page iv of this book to download them.

Alternatively, you could browse to:

https://SmartLeadershipHut.com/tapm-bonus

and download them!

"He" means "She" + "He"

For purposes to make the reading of this book much easier for you, I consistently refer to "He" throughout this book, where, in reality, I mean "She and or He" because, of course, this book is for both women and men. Women procrastinate as much as men do, so women too can benefit tremendously from this book as well as men can. But the readability would become worse in my opinion when you have to read every time he and/or she where at the same time I now refer only to "he." So, please, keep in mind that you, my dear reader, might be equally a woman or a man. And to serve you best with reading this book, I only use the word "He" to refer to both "She" as well as "He." I sincerely hope that I will not offend anyone with this practice.

This book, and the tools I've provided to support you offer the best of everything I've heard, seen, studied, tried, and experienced. It's the best of what I know, all in one life-changing book. And it is simple! Let's get started!

It's an understatement to say that managing myself did not come naturally to me. I had to learn it the hard way so I could teach it to you the easy way. I read everything I could get my hands on about people - psychology books, human behavior books, management books, self-help books.

This book will teach you how to change your Mindset from a Procrastination Mindset into an Anti-

Procrastination Mindset. If you know exactly how to think to be successful, you can optimize your behavior, interactions, and relationships. Trying to cruise through life without a framework is a bit like solving complex math puzzles without any equations. It's both difficult and involves a heck of a lot of unnecessary suffering along the way. This book will give you the mindset you never learned in school. As diverse as we all seem on the outside, our inner workings are quite similar. There are hidden rules to human behavior. We just have to find where to look.

What Is Procrastination?

So, what exactly is procrastination? Well, for me it's quite simple: You have set yourself a goal to perform a certain task. But by the time you actually have to do the task, you are hesitating, unwilling to start, unwilling to feel the discomfort of doing something new or taking a hard decision. Or maybe you feel overwhelmed, and you don't know where to start. In either way, the end result is always the same, you don't do what you are supposed to do. That's procrastinating.

If you don't have goals and you have no activities planned, then there is nothing to procrastinate on. You can only procrastinate when you have a scheduled task but postpone working on it.

It is impossible to procrastinate without goals because there are no planned activities that must be met. At the same time, you might feel "lousy" because you accomplish so little in your life.

So, procrastinating has everything to do with not doing what you have to do to achieve whatever goal you have set for yourself.

30 Signs that you are a Procrastinator

There are many forms of procrastinating. And even much more effects of being a procrastinator. If you can recognize yourself in the various signs of being a procrastinator described below, then chances are that you are one. It may be that you are a high or a low procrastinator. Just check it out for yourself.

Before we proceed, I'd like you to invite to test the level of your procrastination right now. Just to see where you stand right now. It is just a self-assessment to give you an idea of where you stand right now. It is certainly not an absolute figure. And then, after you've implemented the lessons of this book, turn back to this page, and do the same self-assessment again. I promise you that you will discover a jump in your personal development, productivity, and happiness about yourself.

So please, take five minutes to do this test and write down your score and the date of the score, preferably somewhere where you know you can find it back shortly after you have implemented all the lessons of this book.

Below you'll find 30 symptoms of being a procrastinator. Ask yourself how often you'll experience each one of those symptoms. Just think back about the last month or so and then ask yourself for each of the symptoms how often this applies to your life. If it Never applies to you, you give yourself 1 point for the corresponding symptom. If it always applies to you, you give yourself 5 points. Just check the number of points at the top of the checklist. After you have evaluated all 30 symptoms add all the numbers up to a total number which you can fill in the box below the page. This is of course not a black & white objective measure, it is just to give you a feeling of where you stand right now, just before you are starting the adventure of becoming more productive, effective, efficient and happy.

I can imagine that you want to print this checklist out. Therefore, I advice you to download this checklist together with all the other free book bonuses.

Please, use the QR-code on page iv of this book to download them.

Alternatively, you could browse to:

https://SmartLeadershipHut.com/tapm-bonus

and download them!

The Anti-Procrastination Mindset

Procrastination Signs Self Assessment Test

	Never (1)	Rarely (2)	Sometimes (3)	Often (4)	Always (5)	POINTS
1 You are running around without getting anything accomplished.						
2 You find it difficult to get started.						
3 You spend too much time gathering materials "necessary" to start.						
4 Anything can interrupt you while working on a task.						
5 You have a hard time making decisions.						
6 You ignore deadlines.						
7 You avoid tasks if you think that you can't do them.						
8 You waste a lot of time.						
9 You don't feel guilty if you are not getting things done.						
10 You get discourage quickly when faced with long and complex challenges.						
11 Challenges don't motivate you.						
12 You think too easy about how long it takes to complete a particular task.						
13 Having more than one thing to do gives you difficulty to get you going.						
14 You are questioning the point of doing a task.						
15 You spend more time on thinking about the tasks then actually doing the tasks.						
16 You get easily preoccupied with details when you perform a task.						
17 You take more breaks than necessary.						
18 You think that you can always put things off to another time.						
19 You have little accomplished at the end of the day.						
20 You have difficulties doing something you don't want to do.						
21 You end up doing something totally else when you actually should have completed that important task.						
22 You tend to take on more than you actually can handle.						
23 If you are performing a task you are overthinking it with all kinds of what-if scenarios.						
24 You easily back out of things you are involved with.						
25 In order to do something, you need to be in the right mood.						
26 You are great at finding excuses for not doing something.						
27 You have difficulty sticking to a schedule.						
28 You feel easily overwhelmed by the amount of work you have to do.						
29 You often find yourself daydreaming when you are working on a task.						
30 You often wait until the last moment to complete a task.						

TOTAL SCORE:

Apart from these behavioral signs, there are also negative consequences of procrastinating often. Procrastinating often has a negative impact on your self-confidence, career opportunities and relationships with others. Furthermore, procrastinating increases your level of stress resulting in increased chances of hypertension and heart disease, digestive issues, lower immune system, sleeping problems, depression.

If you want to learn how to deal with your procrastination signs, then this is exactly the right book for you! So, please, proceed!

Now, that you know the signs of procrastination, you can become better aware when you are doing it. This is the first step in beating your procrastination. Now, let's have a closer look at what causes your procrastination:

What Causes your Procrastination?

Everyone is different of course, so everyone has its own reasons for procrastinating. You might also have multiple reasons for various occasions. For example, I am often too focused on what I am doing that I completely forget my other tasks and even appointments! Is that procrastinating? Yes, in a way it is, although it is in this case mostly subconscious. Nevertheless, I am responsible for all of my actions and appointments, so it's no excuse. I am also too busy in my life right now to finally start exercising my body in the gym, so I also put that off (for quite some years now!)

This all means that there is not one cause for all procrastination. Conquering your procrastination is a multi-faceted and complex endeavor. Nevertheless, it is also very beneficial, and the return on investment is extremely large! I dare to say, that no other investment in time or money can beat investing in beating your procrastination!

Having said that, let's unpack the complex puzzle called procrastination by first looking at all the reasons why you might procrastinate:

You Are a Perfectionist (aka Fear of Failure)

I am a recovering perfectionist myself, so I don't blame you for it if you are one yourself. But a fact is, that there are a lot of perfectionists among us, and they all tend to procrastinate out of fear to fail. It is like fear of rejection. A lot of people fear to be rejected by someone they like, and therefore they don't dare to approach them. Like they don't dare to perform a particular task, especially when it is something they have never done before. I don't know about you, but I still have difficulties doing new things. And that is always because I am afraid that I am not capable of doing it. I have lost a lot of opportunities in my life because I even did not dare to try to go for it. I vividly remember, when I was 12 years old, my English teacher in High School threw a chalkboard eraser at me. Instead of trying to catch it, I stepped back and let it fall to the ground. I was convinced I couldn't catch it. The reason for this is that I am blind with one eye, so I can't see depth. But, having said that, I didn't even try it! I was too afraid of making a mistake!

You might think, that you protect yourself from failure if you procrastinate. But in fact, you are far worse off. Because now you miss the experience of the action and you have no chance of improving yourself.

So, instead, see yourself as a human being who may make mistakes to improve himself. Don't withhold yourself from experiencing new things! Life is far too short for that! Dare to fail, but do it as quickly as possible. And then learn from it!

Anti-Procrastination Hack:

Dare to make mistakes as quickly as possible and maximize your learnings.

Related to the fear of failure, is the **fear of success**. If you have success, this will set expectations for others, like your stakeholders, relatives or friends. This will raise the bar for future accomplishments. And for someone with a fear of failure, this is very scary. So, that's why people who fear failure, most of the time also will fear success. Another great reason for procrastinating!

What do you think to have Oprah Winfrey, David Beckham, Barack Obama, Donald Trump, Bill Gates, Elon Musk and Steve Jobs in common? Like all successful people, they have an Anti-Procrastination Mindset instead of a Procrastination Mindset. Someone with an Anti-Procrastination Mindset is highly successful because he knows what it takes to achieve goals. Spoiler alert: this means doing the hard work and dealing with obstacles in a constructive way.

In the movie As Good as it Gets, Jack Nicholson plays a misanthropic and obsessive-compulsive novelist, who suddenly realizes that his life will never be any better than the miserable state it is in now. "What if it is as good as it gets?" he realizes himself. That's a perfect example of someone with a Procrastination Mindset. Someone with a Procrastination Mindset accepts the situation he is in right now as the best he can ever achieve in life realizing that it will never be any better. But that's not true. Life is continuously changing, and people can change too, even for the better. Realizing that you have the power to change and to improve your life on any given day, will set you up for success. You only have to believe that there is always room for improvement and that it is up to you to realize that. And you need to motivate yourself to take action. The action which is needed to change the quality of your life for the better. Doing nothing is no option here! You can change your life for the better if you are willing to take action. That's what an Anti-Procrastination Mindset provides you. An Anti-Procrastination Mindset provides you with the attitude and motivation to take action because you believe that you can improve yourself and your life's situation so that you ultimately will be more successful and happy. Don't worry if you have a Procrastination Mindset right now because in this book I'm going to teach you how you too can develop an Anti-Procrastination Mindset!

You are afraid to leave your comfort zone (aka Fear of the Unknown)

Most people are afraid to get out of their comfort zone. I am too! Certainly, when you are developing yourself, you are exploring new things all the time. If you are afraid to explore the unknown because you feel uncomfortable about it, then it is often easier to put it off. You might have all kinds of limiting beliefs about yourself which prevent you from trying new things. And you know what? Most of the time these beliefs are not even true! They are just a figment of your imagination! So, check your beliefs.

A couple of years ago, the whole Tax system in The Netherlands, where I live, was changed. The next year, we all had to comply with the new regulations. At first, I thought that it would be very difficult. A great excuse for procrastinating! But after I found help with a tax consultant, it all appeared to be very simple! What was I thinking!

Doing new things can be scary because you don't know if you can deal with the process as well as the outcome. But does this mean that you should deny yourself new experiences? No, of course not! Do you know what the secret is of highly successful performers like world champion athletes or presenters? Are they not nervous before their performance? Yes, they are! But instead of saying to themselves "I am nervous" they say to themselves "I am excited!!" They give their feeling of nervousness a different more positive meaning. You only have to be aware that both feelings are the flip coin of each other.

Anti-Procrastination Hack:

Say to yourself "I am excited to start this new task" instead of saying that you are nervous or afraid.

Start using this positive affirmation: "I am always excited when I start something new!"

More on positive affirmations and how they help you beat your procrastination, in a later chapter.

You put things off to do it "later" (aka You take the wrong Break)

This is a very nasty one, putting things off to do them later. This often happens either just before you need to start your planned task or when you are halfway and your concentration is gone, or you are tired. You think "Well, this can wait, can't it? It doesn't hurt if I continue writing this report tomorrow. No harm is done when I start tomorrow working this project plan." Sounds familiar? Well, I have used this a lot to soothe my conscience when I didn't feel like it. But ... the comfort of this line of thinking is very temporarily. Earlier than later, your future-self will be banging on your door. And it will be ugly! You are not going to like it! Your future-self will be very disappointed and angry at you because it has reaped all the disadvantages of the little comfort you have had today by putting things off. This is the big gap between your current-self and your future-self. Your future-self knows that not exercising today will turn out negatively in the near and far future. Your current-self only looks at how tired you are.

This gap between your current-self and future-self and the way it causes you to procrastinate has two underlying principles: the **hot-cold empathy gap** and **inconsistency**. Let's dive in:

Everything is perception. Human beings can't perceive reality. Everyone is always looking through a pair of colored glasses. This might be rose-colored glasses or black-colored glasses, or anything in between. In either way, it is a distortion of your reality. The leading expert on willpower, Roy Baumeister, calls this the hot-cold empathy gap. This refers to the two types of thinking we have: hot thinking vs. cold-thinking.

Hot thinking or fast thinking is intuitive, automatic, reactive and experimental thinking. It can help you do things very efficiently and react very quickly in case of emergency. However, hot thinking causes you to jump to conclusions which may not be accurate, and it reinforces your biases. Hot thinking is directed to your present awareness.

Cold thinking or slow thinking is deliberate, controlled, sequential and analytical thinking. It takes a lot of effort, focus, and concentration. It challenges false assumptions and guides you through new situations. At the same time, cold thinking might overwhelm you when you try to process too much information. Cold thinking allows you think about your future-self.

The **hot-cold empathy gap** is a cognitive bias where you underestimate the influence of your hot thinking on your behaviors, attitudes, and preferences. You are dependent on the "state" you are in. So, if you are angry, you can't imagine yourself being calm. When you have drunk a couple of glasses of water, you can't imagine that you were very thirsty, just 10 minutes ago. This is why people sleep a night over an important decision. If you wake up the next day, your hot thinking about the subject is gone, so now your cold thinking can do its thing. Often this results in concluding that things aren't that rose-colored or bad as we thought the day before.

This is how you beat your procrastination! As soon as you want to put something off, take a break! Don't decide yet to put it off or not. Just take a break. Do something different for a couple of minutes, or, even better, take a walk or meditate for 10 minutes. Now, your cold thinking can take it over from your hot thinking. And you can evaluate the decision to postpone your activities to some point in the future and what the impact will be on your future-self. Now you can take a much better decision. If your decision is still to reschedule the activity for another time, then it's no longer a way of procrastinating. Now it has become a strategic decision which fits both your current-self as well as your future-self.

Anti-Procrastination Hack:

Put your urge to put things off on hold. Take a 10-minute break. A mental break! Not a distraction from social media or so! Meditate or take a walk. This gives your cold thinking a chance to step in. What will be the impact on your future-self?

So, don't take the wrong break by seeking distraction on YouTube, Facebook, email or complaining to colleagues. Instead, take the right break by taking a short walk or meditating. This will calm down your hot thinking and gives your cold thinking a chance to step in. Most of the time you will see, your urge to put things off has vanished. You will be re-focused on what you were doing before your short break.

Apart from the **hot-cold empathy gap**, procrastination has another underlying principle: **inconsistency**. Unfortunately, this is something a lot of people suffer from (especially my wife!).

You are not consistent in what you want (aka You don't have a clear Vision)

Inconsistency is the tendency to have different preferences at a specific moment or over time, leading to changing decisions and conclusions.

There are two components of inconsistency: **Internal Friction** and **Time Inconsistency**.

Internal Friction is that there are multiple versions of yourself when you take the decision to pursue a goal. Each version of you represents a different viewpoint. For example, in your role as a parent, you order your kids to go to bed at a certain time. But in the role of the friendly playmate who likes to play with his kids, you might say "Okay, you may stay up for a half hour longer so that we can play that game one more time." These different forces in you make you inconsistent. And your kids know that too! The same applies to pursuing your goals. The goal achiever in you likes to work on your goal and get things done. However, the father, husband, friend or son in you might want to spend his time with his kids, spouse, friend or parents. How do you balance all those forces within you?

Be aware that you play different roles at the same time. You always wear multiple hats. And every hat has another influence on your decisions. Be aware that you always act on multiple levels at the same time. For example, when I am helping my daughter with her homework, I play the role of father and teacher. At the same time, I also have the role of being a husband and son, for example, which also requires my attention. At the same I want my daughter to succeed at school (goal level). But on another value level, I might find it annoying that she didn't put in enough effort to understand her homework herself. This might cause me to interrupt my tutoring suddenly and spend time with my wife. Am I putting things off now? Or is this a strategic choice so that my daughter has the chance to figure it out herself?

If you want to achieve your goals, then the very first step is to be consistent with your goals. And this all starts with being very clear about what you want and don't want. On all levels and for all roles you play.

Anti-Procrastination Hack:

Don't work on anything which is not adding up to a clear goal which excites you. Always start with defining a clear goal which excites you in all roles you play and on all levels.

Time Inconsistency is when you want A today, B tomorrow and C the day after when A and B are completely forgotten. The problem with that is that most goals, especially the more compelling ones, take a longer period of time to complete. For example, writing a project plan, losing a couple of pounds, becoming healthier, and so on, takes at least a couple of weeks and most of the time much longer. If your priorities change every week, you will never achieve any goals. And that's a pity of course.

Changing priorities cause you to lose interest in the activities you have to do, an easy way out to put things off!

Your future-self wants you to decide what is most beneficial for you in the long run. Your current-self, however, tends to overvalue what is beneficial for you right now. If you want to listen to your future-self and become consistent over time, you need to stop your hot thinking and start cold thinking. Instead of worrying about your current-self, start thinking about your future-self. What is the impact of the decisions you make today on your future-self? How do your today's actions and lack of actions contribute to what you value most in life? By the way, what are your most important values?

One of the best ways, as we will see later in this book, is to schedule a daily review meeting with yourself to create a clear direction towards your goals and allow yourself to work on it every day.

People like Warren Buffet and Bill Gates spend a great amount of their time thinking about their life and business. Tim Armstrong (AOL's CEO) takes this even a step further. He makes his executives think about their business 10% of their day. Jeff Weiner (LinkedIn's CEO) schedules even 2 hours of uninterrupted thinking time every day. Why do these famous CEO's spend so much time on thinking? Well, simply because this is the best and only way to get a clear vision and gain direction and focus on your life and business.

If you want to stay focused, then you first need something to focus on. And it better be something important, because your concentration is extremely valuable! To know what to focus on, you need direction. And you get direction by thinking ... a lot! Like in photography, focus has everything to do with vision. So, the first step in creating more focus is to create a clear vision.

Anti-Procrastination Hack:

To beat your procrastination, you need direction and focus. Follow along with successful people and schedule your daily strategic thinking time to create this direction and focus for yourself on a consistent basis.

For every goal, your future-self wants, your current-self has to put in all the work. So, you better balance the interests of your future-self and your current-self. Because all your current-self ever wants, is instant gratification. So, you need to motivate your current-self to delay the need for instant gratification to work on the goals of your future-self. This is done by keeping a clear vision of the end goal in mind. To do that, you first need to develop that clear vision, of course. Furthermore, you need to keep this vision alive, by keeping it in your mind at all time until your goal is achieved.

Anti-Procrastination Hack:

Develop a clear vision of the end goal and keep this vision in your mind at all times. This makes you consistent over time.

You avoid cracking the hard nut

Some people are quite busy accomplishing nothing. They are busy responding to their emails. They run around like headless chickens. They are very actionable and energetic when it comes to doing things, but at the same time, they are lazy thinkers. They don't strategically think about the best next step to take. Let alone that they take the 80-20 principle into account. I don't know about you, but I certainly behave very often like the people I just described. And this is not because I am not capable of thinking strategically, but it simply is because I am procrastinating cracking the hard nut. To give me the illusion of being busy and productive, I start checking my emails and doing some admin work. The problem is that this also gives me a good feeling about myself because of the instant gratification I get from accomplishing all those small tasks. However, in the meantime, I drift away further and further from the real problem I need to solve right then and there. But hey, "I'm human too, you know!"

The reason you avoid cracking the hard nut by running around like a headless chicken is that you don't see the implications on your future-self. No Pain, No Gain! But who wants to feel pain without seeing any gain? Well, nobody, of course. So, if you want to focus on the right things, you need to see the end goal and how this will benefit you.

I don't know if you have ever heard about the Marshmallow Test? If not, just check it out on YouTube. There are lots of amusing clips about this test!

AFTER YOU HAVE FINISHED READING THIS BOOK, OF COURSE!!!

In the late 1960s and early 1970s, Stanford psychologist Walter Mischel performed his famous Marshmallow test. He gave 4-year olds the choice to eat one Marshmallow right now or wait fifteen minutes and then get two Marshmallows. Years later, Mischel checked in on the participants. He found that those kids who had waited the fifteen minutes did better in life in all sorts of ways. The power to take control over oneself and fight distractions seems to be an excellent predictor of success in life. The way these 4- year olds managed to delay their instant gratification, is by keeping the end goal of getting two marshmallows, and how they would benefit from it, in their mind. This is called future-self visualization and will be discussed later in this book.

If you do future self-visualization every day on your goals, then you will probably start to see that you will procrastinate less. This is because you are much more aware of the impact your procrastination has on your future-self. And while you will meet your future-self on a regular basis, you will much more take into consideration what is good for your future-self. So, if you planned to work on one of your goals today, then procrastinating means that you will do your future-self harm and therefore you will start taking action instead.

Anti-Procrastination Hack:

Unknown is Unloved. Perform future-self visualization on a daily basis, so

> *that you come to love your future-self and you no longer avoid cracking the hard nuts because you know and feel that it will harm your future-self.*

You don't feel like doing it (aka You lack motivation)

One of the most common reasons people give why they procrastinate is lack of motivation. Especially for starting unpleasant tasks. Most procrastinators have the misconception that they need to be motivated to begin a task. However, that is a misleading viewpoint.

It turns out that doing is the real motivator. So, you only get motivated by the act of doing. Do you want to feel motivated, just start doing! Taking the first step, regardless of how small, will encourage you to proceed to take the next step and the next step after that. So, one of the tricks to beat your procrastination is to define the best first step. This first step should be so small, that it will only take you a minute or less to perform it. It should be so small, that can't refuse to take it! Another great way to make it easier for yourself to start an activity is to use temptation bundling, as we will discuss later in this book.

Anti-Procrastination Hack:

To get you motivated to start your task, make the very first step as

> small as possible, so that you can't refuse to take it. Identify the tiniest little domino stone, that, when thrown over, will throw over everything else.

Every year, I need to do my taxes, and every year, I manage to postpone this very unpleasant task until the very last hour before the deadline arrives. In the meantime, I have a lot of stress of thinking about this huge task on my To Do List. I will never get motivated to do this task. The only reason I finally manage to do it is that I am forced to by the approaching deadline. And every year, when I finally have started to do my taxes, I think after 20 minutes or so: "Why didn't I start much earlier? It isn't so bad as I thought it was! In fact, it is a piece of cake!

Another question you might ask yourself is why you think that you are not motivated to perform a certain task. Are you self-sabotaging yourself, or not? What do you think exactly when it comes to starting the task? Everything always has advantages and disadvantages. I know, of course, all the disadvantages of doing the taxes. Boring!! But do I also see the advantages? Do I see the end result and how that will benefit me? That's a question you should ask yourself.

If not, then sit down, take a piece of paper and start writing down what exactly the end result is and how it will benefit you. This will fuel your internal motivation. To help you with this, please read the metaphor of the Stonecutter (p.217) and ask yourself which Stonecutter you are?

Anti-Procrastination Hack:

Fuel your internal motivation, by having a clear picture of the end result and how that will benefit you.

You don't know how to do it (aka Your next step is not SMART)

Another reason why you might procrastinate is that you don't know how to start or you lack the skills necessary to complete certain aspects of the task. In this case, thinking of the task will frustrate and confuse you, and while that is an awkward feeling, you avoid thinking about the task, let alone performing the task.

I have often had to perform tasks, I had no clue about how to perform it. Very frustrating! And often it took me a lot of time to find out how to perform it. I remember in University when I got my first programming course in Turbo Pascal! I loved it, but nevertheless, some assignments were simply too complex for me. I always found all kind of excuses not to start working on my assignment. Until I finally had the nerves to ask a fellow student to help me out. When I found out how to perform the first few steps, most of the time I could find my way through until the end. And often also with good results. But what stress!

The key is to break-down the task until you know exactly what to do and to isolate the steps you need help with. And then, of course, ask someone to help you take the next step. In this day and age, this is mostly a very easy step, compared to my college days, because now we have Google.

Anti-Procrastination Hack:

Break-down the task until you know exactly what to do and where to ask help for.

You get easily distracted because the task is too boring (aka You lost track of the big picture)

Performing easy tasks can be boring, and so we get easily distracted! There is always something more fun to do than those lousy, boring tasks! So, let's have a quick look at my Facebook account. Are there any new messages? Speaking of messages, do I have new email? Let's check something on YouTube! And before we know it, we have spoiled an hour or so, with doing irrelevant but pleasant things. That's just a short-term gratification of course! As one of my teachers in college used to say: "You can't win the Nobel Prize every day!" What she meant with this, is that if you want to achieve a big goal, this often means that you also have to do a lot of boring and nasty tasks to get there. But, if you keep the big goal in mind, this should be no problem. The big reward is patiently waiting for you to grab it. This is why it is important to know why you are doing the things you are doing. Even the smallest insignificant task can add up to something big, as you will learn in the metaphor of the stonecutter (p.217). In fact, it is very smart to do something very small which seems insignificant.

Let me tell you why:

If the thing you are doing right now, is in line with what you are doing today, this week, this month, this year, the next five years and ultimately the next 30 years then that's super powerful. Because the thing you are focusing on right now acts like a domino stone, which is lined up to knock over all the next domino stones, even the bigger ones. In fact, a domino can knock over another domino about 1.5x larger than itself. A chain of dominos of increasing sizes makes a kind of mechanical chain reaction that starts with a tiny push and knocks down an impressively large domino. A tiny little domino stone of 5 millimeters has the potential power of knocking over the entire Empire State Building if the next 20 domino stones are lined up correctly.

This is why successful people (aka people with the capability to knock off the Empire State Building) have a life's vision and goals aligned with that vision. And the only thing you have to do every day is to discover the tiny little domino stone you have to push. Boring maybe. But very powerful! And who knows? One day, it might even add up to you winning the Nobel Prize!

11

Anti-Procrastination Hack:

Don't procrastinate on boring tasks. Be aware that even boring tasks can

> *add up to winning the Nobel Prize. Know your overall game plan and how small tasks will relate to that. Without throwing off that first tiny little domino stone, nothing else will be accomplished.*

You think you don't have enough time (aka You fall into the procrastination trap)

It often happens that life gets in the way. Meetings slip, you get all kinds of unexpected phone calls, colleagues are asking you questions, your kids ask for attention, and so on. So, activities you planned can get crushed by the overwhelm of things happening in your everyday life. And instead of 60 minutes left, to perform that important task, you now end up with only 15 minutes left. What do you do? If you are like me, then you probably think that it's not possible to perform the task in 15 minutes, so instead of doing something, you don't do anything for this particular task and goal.

The impact of this line of thinking is that you now have started a track record of procrastinating on this goal. This makes it easier for you to procrastinate the next time again, and the next after that again and again. Don't fall into this procrastination trap!

Every bit of effort you make on any given goal can add up to finally achieving your goal at some point in the future. Doing nothing is no option! Working on a goal for 10 minutes every day can easily add up to the equivalent of a 40-hour work week. This is why I define my daily tasks in sprints of 20 minutes. This helps me to fill in the gaps where I have some time left with doing something useful.

So, do yourself a favor and work on your goals even if you have only 15 minutes left or so. Just find the smallest next step you can find to complete in that short period of time. Even if it is only thinking about your next step, brainstorming and making a mind map or something like that. Everything is better than doing nothing. This way you gain traction for your goal, and you will be better motivated and prepared to work on your goal next time you have a time-frame scheduled to work on it. Furthermore, you will feel good about yourself to have accomplished at least something on your goal. And last but not least, you will not fall into the procrastination trap!

Anti-Procrastination Hack:

Don't fall into the procrastination trap! Don't think that you have not enough time to spend on working on your goal. Even if you have only five minutes left on your agenda, it is better to do something tiny than nothing at all.

Procrastination Causes Self-Assessment Test

Before we proceed, I'd like you to invite to test the level of your procrastination causes, right now, as we did before with the procrastination signs self-assessment test. And then, after you've implemented the lessons of this book, turn back to this page, and do the same self-assessment again. I promise you that you will discover a jump in your personal development and productivity and that you will procrastinate less than ever before.

So please, take five minutes to do this test and write down your score and the date of the score, preferably somewhere where you know you can find it back shortly after you have implemented all the lessons of this book.

Below you'll find 9 possible causes of your procrastination. Just reflect back to the last month or so and think about the times that you procrastinated. How often did you experience each one of those causes?

I suggest that you download a printable version of this self-assessment test and then print it out. Put the date on it and mark for each of the 9 causes how often you think it has occurred. This is of course not a black & white objective measure, it is just to give you a feeling of where you stand right now, just before you are starting the adventure of becoming a more productive and successful goal getter who hardly procrastinates.

You can download the Printable Self-Assessment Test for free. Please, follow the QR-code on page iv of this book.

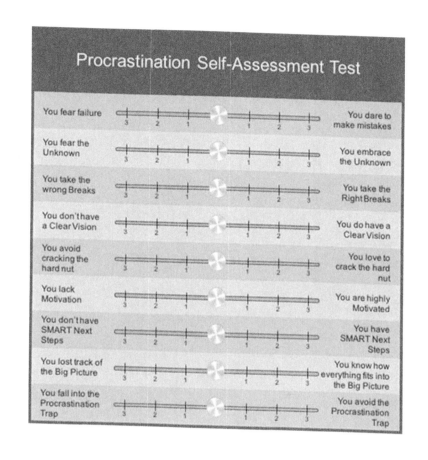

Procrastination Self-Assessment Test

Remember: this is not an absolutely objective figure. It is just an indication of where you stand right now, as opposed to where you will stand after implementing the lessons of this book.

What Causes Your Procrastination?

Take Control of your Reptilian Brain

In the previous chapter, we have discussed 9 causes of your procrastination. But behind those 9 causes, there is one single root cause, and that is your Reptile Brain. This is one of the three brains you, and everyone else for that matter, have in his head. And it is the root cause of all hot thinking. So, whenever you procrastinate or buy or say something on an impulse while regretting it later, it is your reptile brain at work. By understanding your reptile brain better and by learning some cool hacks you can use to control it, you can take back control over your life!

Anti-Procrastination Hack:

Take back control over your life! Get to know your reptilian brain and how to control it, instead of letting your reptile brain control you!

So, what exactly is your reptilian brain?

What is your Reptile Brain?

You probably already have heard that your brain consists of three totally different parts. There is your Reptilian Brain, the oldest part from an evolution perspective, the Limbic Brain and the Neocortex Brain. The latter is the newest part from an evolutionary perspective. Together these three brains are called the Triune Brain Model, a term coined by Dr. Paul D. MacLean. See the picture below:

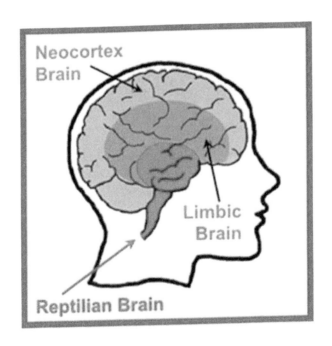

The Reptilian Brain is the part of your brain which deals with basic bodily functions such as pumping your heart, breathing of the lungs, and the regulation of all chemical processes going on in your body. The reptilian brain evolved to serve your genes by driving fundamental needs such as feeding, survival, mating, and self-maintenance.

As you can see, the reptilian brain is responsible for the very basic functionality of you as an "animal." Therefore, the reptilian brain is said to be very primitive and animalistic. Hence, the name of this part of your brain, the reptilian brain, because it closely resembles the brain of reptiles such as lizards. The lizard brain is another synonym for the reptilian brain.

The reptilian brain is part of your subconscious mind, and its primary role is to make sure you stay alive and spread your genes. Therefore, like reptiles, it shows no mercy. You either dominate the others, or you will be dominated by the others.

The reptilian brain does not learn from its mistakes. It only understands images, and it does not understand language. Your lizard brain only has a limited set of behavioral responses which can be triggered by certain external triggers.

Examples of these basic behavioral responses are dominance, aggression, seeking a mate, worship, sex, fear, rigidity, compulsiveness, obsessiveness, greed, and submission. If you would not have your neocortex and limbic system, then you would be like a wild animal defending your territory.

The reptilian brain only understands visual images while the optic nerve is directly connected to your reptilian brain. That's why visualization techniques work so well because this is the best way to influence your reptilian brain.

If you want to have more focus in your life, become a goal getter and stop procrastinating, then the reptilian brain is your best friend. The reptilian brain is the gate-keeper for the attention of the rest of your brain. So, only if your reptilian brain determines that something is worth paying attention to, your subconscious mind, and your conscious mind will have a chance to pay attention to it as well. Again, this is why visualization techniques work so well because they help you channel your mental energy and attention towards your goals.

Anti-Procrastination Hack:

Use Visualization techniques to control your Reptilian Brain because your Reptilian Brain is highly visual.

Pain or Pleasure?

The reptilian brain is concerned with avoiding pain as a means to the survival of the body and the genes. Much more than it is with gaining pleasure. So, if you want to focus your reptilian brain on the task at hand, appealing to the avoidance of pain is more effective than appealing to pleasure.

For example, if I want to be in better shape by exercising more, I can try to motivate myself to go to the gym by thinking of the healthy body I will get. But this doesn't appeal to my reptilian brain at all. So, my reptilian brain will not be focused on exercising. Instead, it will focus on all the other things which ask for my attention. However, if I think of being out of shape and all the negative consequences this will have for me, then I have the attention of my reptilian brain. Now, my reptilian brain will start to focus on going to the gym which makes it easier for me to do it actually.

Positive Visualization and Positive Affirmations can be very powerful as you will see later in this book. However, without focusing first on the pain you can avoid by working on your goal, your reptilian brain will never get focused on your goal. That's why you also need to practice Negative Visualization.

Anti-Procrastination Hack:

Motivate your Reptilian Brain to focus on your goal, by focusing on avoiding the pain first This is done by practicing Negative Visualization.

The Pain-Pleasure Paradox

No Pain No Gain, they say. And yes, that's true. To experience pleasure, you first have to go through a certain level of pain. If you want to have the pleasure of speaking Italian on your next holiday, you first need to study a lot. And that goes together with experiencing pain to some extent. Everyone sees more or less pain in their life, but unfortunately only a few are lucky enough to see pleasure as well. It is a process where you put in the pain first, and where the pleasure is the output.

The paradox of pain vs. pleasure is that most people give up on feeling the pain too quickly so that they never complete the whole process and never get to benefit from the output which is pleasure. Unfortunately, this giving up leads to feeling another new pain. The pain of avoidance and not being successful.

You can break out of this paradox by realizing that feeling pain is not something bad. It is a necessity to experiencing pleasure.

Get in line, and Stay in line!

If you go to, for example, Disney World, then you often have to wait very long for every attraction. What a lot of people do, is after they have waited for 20 minutes or so, leave their line and go for another attraction, only to return later again and to join the very last person in the waiting line. If only, they had waited for 10 more minutes, then the 20 minutes of waiting would not have been wasted!

In real life situations, people do exactly the same thing!

Like the stonecutter in this picture. After a lot of hard work and nearly reaching the source with all diamonds, he gives up because he doesn't believe anymore that he will reach his goal. Instead, realize that success only comes after a lot of hard work, blood, sweat, and pain.

Expect it!

Endure it!

Survive it!

Succeed it!

One of the reasons that you procrastinate, as we have seen earlier, is that you fear the unknown. So, to stop procrastinating, you need to get comfortable with the unknown. Later in this book, you will learn how to tap into your reserve tank and get used to feeling uncomfortable (the real key to willpower).

Anti-Procrastination Hack:

Learn to accept pain as something good, as something which ultimately brings you the pleasure. Expect the pain, endure the pain, resolve the pain.

The Pain – Pleasure Principle

Everything you do every day is motivated by two fundamental desires: the desire to gain pleasure and the desire to avoid pain. Check it for yourself. Just think back to some recent decisions you have made. This might be major decisions like picking a career or buying a house. And it might be a minor decision, like going to the gym or not, or reading a book or not. If you think about your decisions, in which of those two categories do they fall mostly? Is it avoiding pain or seeking pleasure?

Chances are that you see that a lot of your decisions are made to avoid pain. It seems that avoiding pain is a more powerful motivator than gaining pleasure.

Anti-Procrastination Hack:

Motivate yourself to do the things you need to do by checking what the pain is you can avoid by doing them.

What's in it for me?

Your reptilian brain is strictly responsible for its survival. It is by nature self-centered. So, after you have addressed the pain points of not doing the task and achieving your goal, it is time to address the benefits of doing the task you need to do. Even if this task is something you rather not do. For example, doing my taxes is something I'd rather not do. But I must do it because I have to comply with tax regulations. So, in the previous step, I already have addressed the pain points of not doing my taxes, like getting fines and so on. And now, I have to find something positive in doing it. Every disadvantage has its advantage. You only have to look for it. And if you accept the fact that there is an advantage in doing the task, and say to yourself that you are sure that you will find it, you really will find it. They always say that man can't find things in the house and that only women are good at finding things. But strangely enough, in my family, it is the other way around. It often so happens that my wife or daughter lost their cell phone or keys. In a hurry, they start searching the whole house and can't find it. After a while, I decide to help to search. I know that the keys or cell phone, or whatever we are searching for, must be there. That is a given for me. So, I already have a picture of the object in my mind, and with the certainty that they are there somewhere, I start to locate them. And I always find them first! The same applies to finding something positive in the task you need to do. Be certain that there is something positive and find it!

Anti-Procrastination Hack:

Appeal to the self-centered nature of your Reptilian Brain. Answer the question: What's in it for me? Be certain that there is always something positive to find.

Do you see the difference?

The reptilian brain best understands black and white messages: good or bad, fight or flight, pain or pleasure. So, if you want to focus your reptilian brain on the task at hand, so that it actually gets done, use a black and white type of motivation for yourself. The higher the contrast, the better it will come across to your reptile brain.

You can combine this with the primal pain avoiding behavior of your reptilian brain, see earlier in this chapter. If you can motivate yourself in a way that alleviates the pain of not doing the task and contrast this with the benefits of doing the task, then you can be assured that you will have the attention of your reptilian brain.

You often see Before and After Pictures in ads where they promote all kinds of diet pills. They contrast the painful situation of having an unhealthy body with too much fat with the after situation where you will have a healthy and slim body. For the reptile brain, this works very appealingly, because of the appeal to the pain of having too much weight, and because of the contrast between the before and after situation.

Another way of using contrast is to exaggerate the pain of not doing the task or the benefits of doing the task. It is like being on holiday an African country. You walk to the local market, and they start yelling at you that you need to buy something. As soon as you ask how much it cost, they name a price which is 10 times higher than what you would pay normally. Now the negotiations start. You hear $20, and you think "That's way too high" and then you bid $5. Eventually you both agree that the price will be $8. You are very happy because you still have the original price of $20 in your mind. But in reality, you have paid 400% more than you would have paid elsewhere. That is an example of using contrast.

If you think that not going to the gym, will increase your weight at the end of the month with 1 pound, exaggerate it. Say to yourself, that you will at least gain

4 pounds if you don't go to the gym regularly. And if the benefits of going to the gym will be to lose one pound, exaggerate that too. Say to yourself, that you will lose at least 4 pounds if you start to go to the gym. The contrast is now from -4 to +4 equals 8 pounds instead of 2 pounds!

Anti-Procrastination Hack:

Use Contrast to demonstrate the importance of doing the task instead of procrastinating on it.

Make the intangible tangible (aka Show me the money)

Your reptilian brain only understands visual images. It doesn't understand words. So, you have to make the benefits of doing the task and working on your goal, as well as the disadvantages of procrastinating on it, as tangible as possible. Otherwise, you will not get the attention of your reptilian brain. And that means that you will get distracted by all kinds of areas you don't want to be.

While we live in a digital world, the majority of our tasks we need to do, are also hiding in the digital realm. For example, while I write this book on my laptop, it is not visible to the outside world. As soon as I close my laptop, my book is gone, invisible to everyone. No one sees what I'm actually doing while I'm sitting behind my laptop. This probably applies to you too, if you're a knowledge worker. A lot of your tasks are not tangible. You can't see the project plan you are working on. You also can't touch or feel or smell or taste the sales offer you are making for your customer. The only thing you touch and see is your computer. The rest is invisible. This makes it totally not compelling to your reptilian brain. No wonder, you get easily distracted!

So, next time you need to perform a task, and you want your reptilian brain to be focused on it, what do you do? Be creative and find a way to make your task tangible. What you can do, for example, is to take a piece of white paper, and draw a symbol, word, or picture which resembles the task for you. Lay this piece of paper left or right from your computer so that you will always see it with your peripheral vision.

Another thing I always do is to play focus music in the background. I always use the same track of music, so that my reptilian brain is conditioned to pay attention and focus as soon as the music starts to play. If you'd like, you can download the Stay Focused Music Bundle for FREE.

Please, use the QR-code on page iv of this book to download the focus music bundle.

Alternatively, you could browse to:

https://SmartLeadershipHut.com/tapm-bonus

and download it!

Another way is to sit at a different location if you work on a specific project. For example, if you are writing a research paper, you decide to always work in that one particular chair in your study room. Now, you condition your reptilian brain because every time you go and sit in that chair, your reptilian brain will easily focus on your research paper.

Anti-Procrastination Hack:

Make the task you need to perform as tangible as possible. Be creative and give the task a visual, kinesthetic or auditory representation.

Make clear transitions between activities

You have just finished an activity, and now it is time to start a new one to work on another goal of yours. But how do you transition from one activity to another? Most knowledge workers do everything behind their laptop. This means that if I would look at a movie of your typical workday, I would probably see you sitting behind your laptop. And that's all there is to see. What you are actually doing is invisible. See also the previous section where we talked about making your work tangible. So, how would your reptilian brain know that you have started a new activity? It doesn't! That's one of the reasons that you might procrastinate on starting the new activity because there is no clear difference for your reptilian brain.

The reptilian brain is primarily focused on its survival. This means that it will always be very alert to changes to evaluate danger. However, if there are no changes, the reptilian brain will conserve its energy and will stop paying attention. You lose your focus and concentration. And therefore, you tempt to procrastinate. So, to challenge your procrastination temptation, you need to make a clear transition between your former activity and your next.

There are many ways you can do this, for example:

Change the background music you play when working on your next activity. For example, when I do my email I play a CD of Count Basie with an upbeat tempo. When I am working on a project plan, I play a CD of Chet Baker with a more relaxed tempo.

Change the scenery. Try working in another environment if you start to work on your important task. And if that's not possible, try working from another angle at your desk.

Doing this will help you to be more deliberate about what you are doing and working on. So, if I'm working on making a project plan in Microsoft Word and I play Chet Baker, and I sit on my "project plan chair," then it is very hard for me to do something different. Because, if I wanted to answer a few emails in between, for example, this would mean, that I have to change scenery first. Walt Disney used this strategy a lot. He had different rooms with different chairs for various types of thinking. If he wanted to brainstorm, he used another room, then when he wanted to work out one of his ideas into a plan. While I don't have the luxury of having different study rooms, I change my scenery in another way. As soon as I start handling my email, I am going to sit on the chair opposite of me at the same table I'm working on. And I change the background music as well. This takes deliberate action, and it trains my reptilian brain to go and stay in a certain mode of thinking. The end result is that I am much more focused on the activity at hand.

So, be very deliberate about your working environment and the various types of scenery you choose for working on particular types of work.

21

Anti-Procrastination Hack:

Make a clear transition between the tasks you are working on. Especially the task you tend to procrastinate on, need to be distinguishable from the other tasks. For example, use different background music or change the scenery.

Develop an Anti-Procrastination Mindset

As I said earlier, all successful people have an Anti-Procrastination Mindset. Someone with an Anti-Procrastination Mindset is highly successful because he knows what it takes to achieve goals. Spoiler alert: this means doing the hard work and dealing with obstacles in a constructive way.

Do you want to learn how you can develop an Anti-Procrastination Mindset?

I hope you do because Mindset is everything. Everything begins and ends with Mindset. Everything you do in your life is originated in your mind. Every result you get in your life is a direct consequence of the way you think. If you are out of shape right now, then this is due to your Mindset. If you want to get in shape, then you need to change the way you think because that will change the way you feel and behave and that will result in you better in shape. So, everything in your life is controlled by your Mindset. And developing an Anti-Procrastination Mindset means that you will transform from a procrastinator into a goal getter.

Anti-Procrastination Hack:

Mindset is everything. There is no building built, no victory won, and no world record was broken without the

> *initial necessary spark that started in someone's mind.*

What is Mindset?

"You become what you believe."

- Buddha

The way you think about things, dictate how you will feel about it. And the way you will feel, dictate which actions you will take and which actions you will not take. And the result of all your actions and in-actions determine whether or not you will be successful in achieving your goals. So, if you want other results in your life, you need to change the way you think about things. This is in essence what Mindset is. Your Mindset within a given context determines your perceptions and the way you think about things.

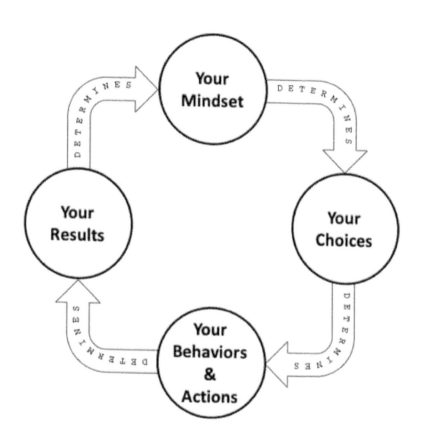

As you can see in this diagram, your Mindset determines your Choices. The way you think about things, the way you see yourself playing all kinds of roles in your life determines whether or not you choose to perform a certain action. So, for example, I see myself as someone who doesn't smoke and who doesn't drink alcohol. So, it will never ever come to my mind to pick up a cigarette, or a glass of wine. Never. This is for me way outside "my world." The table in front of me could be full of packs of cigarettes, bottles of wine and beer, and I wouldn't even notice it. I probably would ask the host of the party if he had something to drink for me. So, subconsciously, I already made a choice not to smoke any of the cigarettes lying on the table waiting for someone to pick them up. As well as I've made the subconscious choice not to drink any of the alcoholic drinks which are standing on the table in front of me. My conscious awareness hardly notices it. This subconscious choice leads to my behavior of asking the host of the party to give me something to drink with which I mean water or any kind of non-alcoholic beverage. And this automatically leads to the result of me not having a hangover and not getting drunk and staying mentally clear all night. And this strengthens my mindset that I am a non-smoker and non-alcoholic-drinker.

Do you see how this works?

If your Mindset leads you to believe that you are too old because you are older than 50 years, then you might draw the conclusion that this means that you can't change jobs and can't start a new career. You will never change careers, even if you get fired in your current job. Probably, you will desperately try to get the same job back with another company. There are thousands of types of jobs, so why limit yourself to this one particular job? What if you pick another job, and you will be successful?

Your Mindset may serve you well for a certain period of time, but as soon as it is not applicable anymore, you have to change your Mindset.

Knowing how to change your Mindset can change you from a Procrastinator into a highly effective and successful Goal Getter. That's why I will give you several tools in this book for you to change your Mindset:

- Results-thinking
- Process-thinking
- Creating and Using a Vision Board
- Controlling your Values Hierarchy
- Future-Self Visualization
- Positive Affirmations

What is The Anti-Procrastination Mindset?

In the movie As Good as it Gets, Jack Nicholson plays a misanthropic and obsessive-compulsive novelist, who suddenly realizes that his life will never be any better than the miserable state it is in now. "What if it is as good as it gets?" he realizes himself. That's a perfect example of someone with a Procrastination Mindset. Someone with a Procrastination Mindset accepts the situation he is in right now as the best he can ever achieve in life. He thinks that life will never be any better than it is right now.

But that's not true.

Life is continuously changing, and people can change too, even for the better. Realizing that you have the power to change and to improve your life on any given day, will set you up for success. Only when you believe that there is always room for improvement and that it is up to you to realize that, you will be motivated to take action. The action which is needed to change the quality of your life for the better.

Doing nothing is no option!

You can change your life for the better if you are willing to take action. That's what an Anti-Procrastination Mindset provides you. This is also called an Anti-Procrastination Mindset as opposed to the Procrastination Mindset.

An Anti-Procrastination Mindset provides you with the attitude and motivation to take action because you believe that you can improve yourself and your life's situation so that you ultimately will be more successful and happy.

How do you know if you have a Procrastination Mindset or an Anti-Procrastination Mindset?

Well, hopefully, you have already performed the two Self-Assessment Tests. If not, I strongly suggest, that you do them now:

- The Procrastination Signs Self-Assessment Test

- The Procrastination Causes Self-Assessment Test

Don't worry if you have a Procrastination Mindset right now because you too can change this into an Anti-Procrastination Mindset. I will show you how in the rest of this chapter.

Anti-Procrastination Hack:

Be aware that a Procrastination Mindset is making it easy for you to

> *procrastinate because you think that putting in the effort is useless anyway. Instead, adopt The Anti-Procrastination Mindset that will change your way of thinking from a procrastinator into a highly successful goal getter.*

Say goodbye to your Procrastination Mindset

Do you have a Procrastination Mindset right now? If you have, you believe that intelligence can't be changed. This way of thinking leads to a desire to look smart. However, you avoid challenges and obstacles, and you tend to give up easily. You procrastinate a lot. You see the effort as pointless. Why bother? And you ignore constructive criticism. Furthermore, you feel threatened by the success of others.

With a Procrastination Mindset, you achieve much less than what you are really capable of.

So, do you have a Procrastination Mindset? Well, I hope not, for you. I can't blame you because I have suffered from a Procrastination Mindset myself. In fact, I'm still recovering from a Procrastination Mindset!

Anti-Procrastination Hack:

Be aware that your Procrastination Mindset is withholding you from being successful in every area of your life. Ditch it asap!

Say hello to your Anti-Procrastination Mindset

According to Stanford psychologist Carol Dweck, your potential is unknown. It is impossible to foresee what you could accomplish in five years from now with passion and training and by doing the hard work. Your level of achievement in a few years' time is not dependent on your intelligence. It is dependent on whether you have a Procrastination Mindset or an Anti-Procrastination Mindset.

An Anti-Procrastination Mindset is the belief that you can grow. Therefore, it is also called Anti-Procrastination Mindset. You believe that intelligence can be developed. This way of thinking leads to a desire to learn. You embrace challenges. You persist in the face of obstacles. If you have an Anti-Procrastination Mindset, you see the effort as a path to mastery. You accept constructive criticism, and you use it to your advantage. When you have an Anti-Procrastination Mindset, you feel inspired by and learn from the success of others. As a result, you will fulfill your optimal potential.

So, do you have an Anti-Procrastination Mindset? I hope you have an Anti-Procrastination Mindset because that would mean that you find success in doing your best, learning and improving. You find setbacks motivating, and you take charge of the processes that bring success.

Anti-Procrastination Hack:

Start to develop an Anti-Procrastination Mindset. This will help you to change your way of thinking so that you will get more focus and clarity on your path to success and the drive to follow through on it.

When I was in University, I attended psychology classes. I learned that psychology was formed over the period of the last 100 years or so by experimenting and testing. In fact, every statement done in psychology was driven by statistics. For example, a psychologist state that people with a Procrastination Mindset believe that their intelligence can't be developed. He would only make such a statement after having researched hundreds of people and after having found the same characteristics over and over again. I concluded that whatever a psychologist says, it must be true because every statement was scientifically proven.

At the beginning of my career, I was asked to do a psychological test, which was a sort of personality test. I was certain that the outcome of this test would describe me as the person I was and always would be. Psychologists can't be wrong, right? The result of the test would be as good as it gets.

How stupid could I be!! My conclusion was not true of course. The test result was only a reflection of me at that moment in time. But it did for sure not mean that I would not be able to develop myself.

It is like the grades you get at school. Do they define you? No! They are only a reflection of the state of your knowledge at that time, certainly not something to live up to.

So, do not believe that your qualities are carved in stone. This belief would create a self-fulfilling prophecy of you proving yourself over and over again as I did to myself. Unfortunately! Instead, start to believe that everything is mutable. Even your brain changes every second of the day in form and nature. So, everything is fluid. Nothing is set in stone. Every moment in time, you can start to make new choices leading to new results.

26

Anti-Procrastination Hack:

Don't believe that your future is carved out in stone because it is not. Instead, your future is malleable. The big question for you is, if you want to shape your future yourself or that you let it shape by sheer randomness.

You can develop your basic qualities, even your basic personality, by cultivating your efforts. That's what The Anti-Procrastination Mindset is about. Everyone is different. Everyone has a different background, innate talent, intellect and so on. And everyone can change. You can change and grow through experience.

Don't quit and don't give up on your way to achieve your goals. Sure, you will have your setbacks. An extreme example of someone with an Anti-

Procrastination Mindset is Elon Musk. With his companies Tesla, Space X and The Boring Company, he had to deal with extreme setbacks continuously. Several times he experienced failures which cost him personally billions of dollars. But do you think that this would cause him to give up? No, because he has an Anti-Procrastination Mindset and he is learning from his failures. It is this Anti-Procrastination Mindset that will make you stand up after you have fallen and which will throw you right back in the race where you were before you fell. An Anti-Procrastination Mindset will motivate you to pursue your goals until you have completed them.

Anti-Procrastination Hack:

Never give up on your goals! Expect setbacks to come your way. Get up. Learn from them. Follow through on your goals until you have achieved them.

Benefits of developing an Anti-Procrastination Mindset

Developing an Anti-Procrastination Mindset can be the best thing you can do for yourself in your life. It will benefit you in numerous ways. I will show you the 6 most beneficial ones for you. So, please read on if you'd like to know how an Anti-Procrastination Mindset can change your life:

It's not your intelligence, stupid

In a study of Carol Dweck, one group of students got fairly challenging problems from a nonverbal IQ test. The students were praised for their performance, like "Wow, you got 70% right. That's a really good score. You must be *smart* at this." Another group of students got the same test but were praised slightly different: "Wow, you got 70% right. That's a really good score. You must have *worked really hard*."

So, the first group of students was praised for their intelligence, and this pushed these students right into a Procrastination Mindset. This was shown later on when these students were given a choice: they rejected challenging new tasks, although they could learn from them. The second group of students, however, was praised for the effort they had made. This pushed them into an Anti-Procrastination Mindset. Most of these Anti-Procrastination Mindset students (90%) wanted to take on new challenges from which they could learn.

It's not that The Anti-Procrastination Mindset group of students were less intelligent than the Procrastination Mindset group of students. It is also not that they were able to put in more effort than the other group. No. It's all a matter of focus. The Anti-Procrastination Mindset group of students were primed to focus on *effort rather than intelligence*. The Procrastination Mindset group of students were primed to focus on their *intelligence rather than the effort*. So, it's all a matter of having the right focus. So, you can change your Mindset from a

Procrastination Mindset into an Anti-Procrastination Mindset. You only have to change your focus.

When both groups of students got an IQ test with a set of harder problems, it turned out that the Procrastination Mindset group of students, who were praised for their intelligence, thought that they were not so gifted after all. If success equals intelligence, then failure means deficiency! For The Anti-Procrastination Mindset group of students, the set of harder problems was only a sign that they had to put in more effort.

Do you see the big difference between both types of Mindset with regards to procrastinating versus not procrastinating?

Benefits of having an Anti-Procrastination Mindset

There are several benefits of overcoming your procrastination by developing an Anti-Procrastination Mindset:

(1) You are more realistic in focusing on doing the hard work. This means that the chances of you doing the hard work are much higher than when you have a Procrastination Mindset.

(2) You are much more flexible, and you will be much more adaptive to changed situations. While change is inevitable in life, the person who is the most adaptive will be the most successful.

(3) You will be more aware of opportunities and possibilities you would never have noticed otherwise.

Your subconscious mind uses your mental filters to filter out 99.99% of all the input it gets because your conscious mind can only deal with 7 plus or minus 2 things at the same time. So, if you have a Procrastination Mindset then why bother your conscious mind with new opportunities? So, they are filtered out for you by your subconscious mind. But if you would have an Anti-Procrastination Mindset, then these opportunities become suddenly interesting because you can do something with them and apply them to achieving your goals. So, now your subconscious mind will elegantly present you all kinds of new opportunities you would otherwise have missed out on.

(4) As we have seen earlier in this book one of the reasons that you procrastinate are:

- You avoid cracking the hard nut
- You don't know how to do it (aka Your next step is not SMART)

Developing an Anti-Procrastination Mindset will be a solution for both problems because you will start to see new opportunities and possibilities that you did not see earlier.

(5) You will be much more open to yourself and to other people when you have an Anti-Procrastination Mindset.

This will solve your Fear of Failure and your Fear of the Unknown. You are willing to admit failures to yourself and to others because you know that this is the best way for you to learn and to improve yourself. Because of that, you will learn faster from your experiences. If you can acquire new skills very fast, then you will be much more successful in achieving your goals and dreams.

At the same time, you will celebrate your successes more because you know that you have earned it by putting in all the hard work and overcoming all the obstacles on your way to achieving that success. Because of that, you will appreciate your hard work more, and that will create the seed for future successes.

(6) You are realistic about all the obstacles you will meet on your path towards your goal. So, you won't become frustrated, depressed, and lethargic at the very first obstacle. Instead, you will be optimistic about achieving your goal and struggle on. This will make you unstoppable, successful and also happier.

(7) You will be much more responsible for your life. Instead of complaining and moaning and groaning of whatever fails in your life or your work, you will be in control of what is happening because you know that you can develop yourself continuously. This will free up a lot of mental energy, and it will focus all your attention towards the tasks you need to complete.

Value the Effort you put in more than the Results you get

We all have learned that you need to set targets for yourself. Otherwise, you would look like a ship without a captain or a car without a driver. And you don't want that, do you? Of course not, because how would you otherwise know that you are going in the right direction? And how could you otherwise evaluate the effectiveness of your day?

So, setting targets is good, but it can also limit you. It can force you into a Procrastination Mindset which will increase the chance of procrastinating.

So, yes, it is good to set targets for yourself upfront and make a plan to accomplish your goals. But immediately after that, you must manage yourself on doing the work.

If your goal is to lose 10 pounds in the next 30 days and your plan is to workout 10 minutes every day to accomplish that, then this daily exercise should become your primary focus. Don't stand every day on the scale to check how many pounds you have lost! This will make you crazy and demotivate you from doing the work. Instead, only focus on your daily effort of doing your work out in the knowledge that every work out will bring you nearer to your goal. And if you have achieved to work out for 30 days in a row, then you may be very proud of yourself! This is a considerable achievement no matter what your scale "says."

It is all a matter of having the right focus. Do you like to focus on something you can't control directly, like "the number on the scale"? Or do you rather focus on something which you can control, like the number of minutes you work out every day? Which of the two, do you think, will be more motivating on a consistent basis so that you keep going?

Anti-Procrastination Hack:

After you have set your goals, don't focus on them anymore. Instead, focus on the effort you need to put in to achieve your goals.

Treat the Results you get as a Measure of your Effectiveness

Having an Anti-Procrastination Mindset means that you value effort over results, as we have seen above. Detach yourself emotionally from the results you get. The only thing that matters is the efforts you have put in. There is, however, one way in which your results can benefit you. Use your results as a measure of your effectiveness.

Let's assume that your master plan is to lose 10 pounds in one month by exercising 10 minutes every day. Now, 30 days later, you have worked out every day. So, you may be very proud of your efforts, because you followed your plan to the letter. Now, if you check your results and see on the scale that you only lost 2 pounds, then don't be disappointed in yourself. There is really no need for that. Detach yourself emotionally from this result. Don't value this result as good or bad. It is just a measure which teaches you something about what the effect is on your workouts.

Every effect has its causes. An effect, however, is something you can't influence. However, you do have control over the causes. So, be proud of yourself that you have executed your master plan perfectly. And let this result be a measure of the effectiveness of your master plan.

So, apparently, 10 minutes' workout every day leads to a loss in weight of 2 pounds after 30 days. So, if you want to lose 10 pounds in 30 days, then you have to work out 50 minutes every day. Now, you can decide if this is something you can realistically apply to your daily routine. If you do have the time and energy to work out 50 minutes every day, then great. Now you know that you are capable of doing the work if you set your mind to it. So, focus on it for the next 30 days and then evaluate the results. If, however, 50 minutes' workout every day is not realistic for you, then change your goal. Don't try to lose 10 pounds in 30 days, because that is not realistic. Instead, aim for losing 10 pounds in 100 days.

Anti-Procrastination Hack:

Be the cause of your results. You can't control your results. You only can control the efforts you take to get to the results. See the result you get only as a measure of the effectiveness of your efforts and nothing more than that. Learn from your results and if necessary, course correct. At all costs, do not let yourself down based on the results.

How to be happy even when your results suck

When you start a new project, you make assumptions about how much progress you will have made after a certain period of time. For example, one month, two months and so on. But what if you are not on target after one month? Will this let you down? Will you stop the entire project? Will you give up on your goal? Or even worse, what if, at the start of your project, you are afraid that you will not achieve the goal you have set after one month, two months and so on? Will you start your project anyway, or give up immediately without even trying? You see, that's the problem of focusing on achieving goals, instead of focusing on the work you have to do every day to achieve your goals.

If you have a procrastination Mindset, you probably will be blinded by the goal you have set and fall into the trap of fearing the failure. So, change your Mindset! Change it into an anti-procrastination Mindset. Don't get yourself scared upfront by the goals you need to achieve and don't let yourself down by the results you got afterward. Instead, see your goals and results as a measure to evaluate the assumptions you have made with regards to the way you progress toward your goals.

Develop an Anti-Procrastination Mindset

It's not about the results you get, it's about how much effort you have put in, to achieve your goals.

Most people, like me, are driven by goals. You set a goal, and then you get fixated on the target. It's like the example I gave you about wanting to lose 2 pounds. Don't get me wrong; it is good to set goals. They give you direction in your life. But as soon as you have set them, you need to focus on the work you need to put in to achieve those goals. So, in this case, you need to focus on working out and eating healthier. That's something you can control. What the scale "says," you can't control. So, why focus on something you can't control?

Being successful doesn't come from setting the right goals and focusing on it. Instead, people who are highly successful aren't focusing on their goals at all. They focus on all the work they need to put in to achieve the success they want. Most of the time, we want quick results because we don't like to do the work and we want instant gratification. However, that is the way of thinking of someone with a Procrastination Mindset. Don't try to control the things, you can't control. That's an illusion. And that is a pity because you focus on the wrong things. You better focus on the things you can control. That's why you need to be realistic about the effort you can put in and adapt your goals accordingly.

When writing this chapter, for example, I don't focus on the deadline and the number of words and quality this chapter should have. Sure, I have set a goal, but I don't focus on it because I know that achieving a goal is just a byproduct of the writing process. So, I only focus on the process of writing this chapter. The reason I have set a goal is to evaluate later if my assumptions were correct so that I can course correct for the next time, if necessary.

I believe that if you start focusing on effort instead of results, you will be not only much happier but at the same time also more successful. Focusing on effort instead of results gives you control, and that's something everyone likes to have. I can control how much I work out every day. Is it 10 minutes, 20, or 30? I can also control how much I eat per day. Furthermore, I can evaluate my day based on the effort I have put in. So, did I really work out 20 minutes as I promised to do? And did I really eat as healthy as I promised myself to do? If yes, then I can be very satisfied with myself because I did what I promised myself to do.

Now, here comes the trick! If I did exactly work out as I promised to do, for a whole month, and eat as healthy as I promised to do, then I can be very proud and satisfied about myself, or can't I? No matter what the scale "says" at the end of the month? Yes, that's right. So, when I stand on the scale at the end of the month, and it happens to be that I lost only 1 pound instead of 2, now what? Should I beat myself up! Should I be disappointed? Should I be frustrated, feeling hopeless and say "Why is this happening to me?" all because I didn't lose 2 pounds as I thought it I would? No, of course not!

If you don't get the results from the work you have put in, it only means that your expectation was based on the wrong assumptions. If you assumed that eating healthier and working out for 20 minutes every day, leads to losing 2 pounds in one month, then now you know that this was a wrong assumption. So, what you can learn from this is, that you need two months to achieve your goal, or that you should have worked out 40 minutes per day to get the same result within one month. But, what's done is done. So, now you can course correct based on the learnings. And you should still be proud and happy about yourself because you have put in all the work you promised to do. The only thing that went wrong is that your assumptions were not correct. But hey, that happens all the time!

To make it real and easy for you, I invite you to follow the steps below, so that you too can become more successful and happy.

Don't believe me?

Just try it out for yourself! What do you have to lose?

So, to develop and strengthen your Anti-Procrastination Mindset, so that you will be happier and more successful, follow these steps:

1) Realize that setting goals give you direction in your life, which is good. But it doesn't predict the outcome of that direction.

2) Realize that every prediction about the outcome is an assumption. You can only test that assumption by putting in the work and then evaluate afterward.

3) Decide on your evaluation period, for example, one month.

4) Plan the work you want to put in for the next period. Set a goal based on the planned effort and assumed progress.

5) Evaluate after one month:

Based on the one month result you got, check if your progress-assumptions are right. If not, adapt them.

 - Repeat the cycle from step 4.

Having an Anti-procrastination Mindset means that you know that you can always achieve more than you think you are capable of right now if only you put in the work to achieve it. The focus, as said earlier, should not be on your results. Results are only a reflection of the work you have put in to get to those results. Instead, you should focus on putting in the effort. Be the cause of your effects and results. So, your focus should be effort based.

Anti-Procrastination Hack:

Take control over the effort you put in to achieve your goals. Evaluate after a period of time, how you have performed, based on the results you got. Use the results only to evaluate your previously made progress assumptions.

Don't blame anyone but yourself when you don't hit your goal

If you set goals, you expect results, of course. But what do you do, when your results are disappointing? Do you course correct? Or do you start complaining or even blaming others for the bad results you got? Often people with a Procrastination Mindset do the latter. They are too focused on the results of a project. They stand, for example, every day on the scale to see if they already have lost their two pounds. That's not only frustrating, but this also brings danger to the chance of actually realizing that goal.

Blaming others for anything that goes wrong in your life, is what seems almost like the norm. Everyone does it. But that doesn't mean that you should do it too. The reason is that it won't help you in any way and it will not do you any good.

In the movie Legally Blonde 2, Reese Witherspoon as the character Elle Woods gives a speech for the members of the Congress, and she uses the metaphor of getting a really bad haircut in a chic hair salon in Beverly Hills. After realizing that the haircut had gone totally wrong, she was angry. But soon, she realized that her anger was completely misdirected. It still was the salon's fault, of course, to give her a bad haircut, but she had also sat there and witnessed this to happen to her. But she wasn't involved in the process. She forgot to speak up! So, instead of blaming the hair salon, she actually had to blame herself!

Don't act like if you are the victim because you are not. Don't blame others because that brings you nowhere.

If you blame someone else or complain about a situation, then you don't take accountability for your situation. Instead, you make someone else accountable for your situation. In reality, you can't make anyone else responsible for your life other than yourself. So, if you choose to make someone else responsible anyway, you are misleading yourself and withholding yourself from going on. This will keep you stuck. Instead of moving on, you procrastinate. To get unstuck in your life, the first step is to stop blaming others and start giving yourself the highest accountability for yourself, as Elle Woods did. So, if you don't get the results you want or expect, ask yourself what you have done so far to get the results you got now. Then ask yourself what you can do to change your behavior to get other results.

Another problem with blaming is that it negatively programs your mental filters. This means that instead of seeing opportunities, you will focus more and more on problems and failures caused by others. This will move you further and further away from the real issue you have to work on, which is getting yourself together and starting to work on your projects.

As soon as you start blaming others, complaining, and whining, you have the perfect excuse to do nothing and to procrastinate. That's not what you want, of course. Why else would you read this book? So, stop it. Become aware of every time you are seeking excuses, complaining, or blaming others. And as soon as you hear yourself doing it, ask yourself, "Okay, but what could I have done differently? What is my role in this? What else does this mean?"

Anti-Procrastination Hack:

Be aware that complaining about a situation or blaming others is just an excuse to procrastinate. Stop it! Instead, ask yourself what you could do differently to get better results and course correct.

Don't expect results too quickly

What happens when you have too high expectations of the results you want to achieve? You will be disappointed. You will be discouraged. You are going to doubt yourself. Probably you think: "Why bother? I will never make it. It is useless to begin anyway."

If you want to see results too quickly, you expect too much of yourself and too fast. The reality will then automatically and by definition disappoint you. You will stop trying to do something because you have realized that you can't succeed. You will throw in the towel. Then you are going to do precisely the opposite of what you should do. You either procrastinate on doing what you have to do, or you give up your goal entirely.

So, don't expect results too quickly!

It is also useless to expect results too quickly because things just need their time. That is a law of nature. That applies to everyone, including you.

Chinese Bamboo Trees don't seem to grow in any way after you have planted them. In the first four years, after planting, you will not see any visible sign that there is a Bamboo tree growing. Finally, in the fifth year, suddenly in six weeks' time, the tree will grow 80 feet. Unbelievable! They can grow so fast because they have laid a solid foundation in the first four years.

The same law of nature applies to you as well. First, you need to invest in doing the hard work without seeing any results. So, instead of focusing on results, you need to focus on laying the foundation first. If you would focus on results, you would probably give up way before you have seen any results. So, you need to trust the process and in the meantime, keep doing the hard work.

There are two main reasons why someone is expecting results too quickly.

(1) You are impatient because you don't want to put too much work into achieving your goals.

For example, you want to lose weight quickly. Then you'd rather be ready tomorrow than the day after tomorrow because the sooner you can forget about your weight loss the quicker you can get on with your life.

You want to get rid of those extra pounds as quickly as possible with as little effort as possible. After all, you do not like to have to work too hard. So, the sooner you have results, with as little effort as possible, the better it is.

(2) You want to self-sabotage yourself. If you expect results too fast, what many people do, means asking for trouble. Firstly, it is an illusion, and it is a mechanism to make it easy for you to give up. If you know that you have to do something, which is not possible, then you know that it is doomed to fail. But if it is consciously or unconsciously your intention to sabotage your plan, then it is, of course, useful to create high expectations, because that is the ultimate recipe for failure.

How can you prevent yourself from falling into the trap of wanting to see results too quickly?

Be realistic. Realize that it is a natural law that everything needs its own pace and time to be accomplished. See the example of the bamboo trees. It is a law of nature that you will always encounter obstacles. No matter how good you are at planning.

"It is a law of nature that you must do difficult things to gain strength and power. As with working out, after a while, you make the connection between doing difficult things and the benefits you get from doing them, and you come to look forward to doing these difficult things."

— Ray Dalio

My wife always expects things to go faster. So, if she wants to clean the house, for example, she hopes to be ready in 1 day, while it would generally take a week or so. Then after a couple of hours, she realizes, that she has only done a fraction of what she expected to have done. Then she panics and ends up doing nothing anymore.

Let go your idea of the result. Make sure you don't think about it when you are starting a new activity. Change your focus. For example, you say to yourself: "I want to clean the house for 2 hours, and I will see how far I have come." So instead of focusing on the result, you focus on the work that needs to be done and then you will check what you have accomplished or not.

Okay, by now, I hope you are convinced that it is much healthier for you to focus on the work that needs to be done and to let go of your idée fixe of the result you want to get. But now what? Can you really let go your hopes for big results?

I need to do administrative work, for example. Well firstly, I don't want to do it, and I want to postpone it as far as possible. But secondly, I want it to be done as quickly as possible. I know that I need to let go of this idea of having it done quickly. So, I say to myself, "The next hour, I will do my administrative work, and after the that I know how far I got." But that is easier said than done. In the meantime, while I finally work on my administrative work, I only think, when am I done? I hope that it is finished quickly. So, I can't let go of this idée fixe of completing it as soon as possible.

The solution to letting go of your idée fixe of wanting to get results too quickly while you know that you want to focus on doing the work is a **"Visual Squash."**

A **Visual Squash** is an NLP technique with which you can "re-wire" your brain. You integrate different parts of your brain which are working like a standalone-island by creating new neural pathways between them. You use your body as a vessel to create those new neural pathways.

1. Think of your idée fixe of wanting to have results too quickly.

2. Hold both your hands in front of you with the palms right up.

3. Make a visual representation of the part of you which is focusing on having results too quickly. Place this visual representation on one of your hands in front of you. How does it look? How does it feel? Warm, cold, heavy, light?

4. Make another visual representation of the part of you which wants to focus on doing the work. Place this visual representation in your other hand. How does it look like? How does it feel? Warm, cold, heavy, light?

5. Go to your first hand. Ask the part on that hand which purpose it has for you. Repeat this question a couple of times until you get the highest purpose of this part.

6. Repeat the same with the other hand.

7. Conclude that both parts actual wants the same for you and they are both parts of an integrated oneness in you.

8. Now bring both hands slowly together. Let your body do its work. As soon as you have concluded that both parts are one of a kind, your body automatically will start moving your hands together. Let it do its job.

9. As soon as your hands have come together, bring them both to your chest, and say "Thank you [your name]"; so, in my case, I say to myself "Thank you, Harry."

Anti-Procrastination Hack:

Don't expect results too quickly. It's unrealistic and counterproductive. It's a way to self-sabotage yourself. Instead, focus on the work which needs to be done and let go of your expectations of the result you will gain from that. Use the **Visual Squash** *technique to help you with that.*

Dare to make mistakes and make them as quickly as possible

Making mistakes is a fact of life. They are inevitable on your way to success. So, you better learn to love them and embrace them. And then learn from them. Failures can be very valuable when you learn from them. Hiding your weaknesses as people with a Procrastination Mindset tend to do, will bring you nowhere. Because then you will probably make the same failure again. And again. So, acknowledge your failures. Or, as Benjamin Zander used to say to his students when they make a mistake: "How fascinating!!!" This is a perfect example of someone with an Anti-Procrastination Mindset because he thinks that growth is always possible if you also dare to make mistakes. That's why Mr. Zander, who is the musical director of the Boston Philharmonic Orchestra and the Boston Philharmonic Youth Orchestra and also teaching at the New England Conservatory, gives his students a straight A at the beginning of each year. "It is a possibility to grow into" he explains it. The best way to become successful is to improve yourself continuously by learning from your failures.

Unfortunately, when you have a Procrastination Mindset, you think that you don't dare to make mistakes. That's not necessarily because you are a perfectionist, but it is mainly because you tend to be ashamed of making failures because you think that making failures says something about you as a person. You identify yourself with the mistakes you make.

I am recovering from a Procrastination Mindset myself, so I don't blame you for it if you have one too. A lot of people fear to be rejected by someone they like, and therefore they don't dare to approach them. Like they don't dare to perform a particular task, especially when it is something they have never done before.

I don't know about you, but I still have difficulties doing new things. And that is always because I am afraid that I am not capable of doing it. I have lost a lot of opportunities in my life because I even did not dare to try to go for it. I vividly remember, when I was 12 years old, my English teacher in High School threw a chalkboard eraser at me. Instead of trying to catch it, I stepped back and let it fall to the ground. I was convinced I couldn't catch it. The reason for this is that I am blind with one eye, so I can't see depth. But, having said that, I didn't even try it! I was too afraid of making a mistake!

You might think, that you protect yourself from failure if you don't try out new things. But in fact, you are far worse off. Because now you miss the experience of the action and you have no chance of improving yourself. So, instead, see yourself as a human being who may make mistakes to improve himself. Don't withhold yourself from experiencing new things! Life is far too short for that! Dare to fail, but do it as quickly as possible. And then learn from it!

When you have a Procrastination Mindset, you are not focused on doing the work necessary to achieve your goals. To hide this, you try to hide the failures you make. People with a Procrastination Mindset think that the level of their intelligence is a fact as something which cannot be changed. In fact, they see the quality of their whole life as something unchangeable. And according to the study of Carol Dweck, it turns out that these people are more likely to mask or hide their failures from others than people with an Anti-Procrastination Mindset. They don't want to look stupid to others. However, if you would have an Anti-Procrastination Mindset, you would know that you never look stupid when you make mistakes. On the contrary, you would know that the more failures you make, the more you would learn and grow and eventually the quicker you would achieve success in accomplishing your goals.

Develop an Anti-Procrastination Mindset

"Making failures is just a way

to find your path to your goal."

Only when you are lucky, you will find the perfect way to your goal the very first time you try. But the chance of that is probably the same as the chance of you winning the lottery. So, it is a fantasy to think that you will not make failures. And it is the most significant mistake of your life when you will give up on the very first failure. Instead, you need to be realistic. Realize that you probably have to try numerous ways before you have found the perfect way to achieve your goal.

In 2008, we were on holiday in Croatia, and one day we were up in the mountains and got off track too much. Finally, we got totally lost in the woods with our car which is totally not an SUV type of car, so totally not suited for the job anyway. Below you can see a picture of our car at the end when we got finally back in the valley. But before it came that far, we first had to find our way back down the mountain. But in the woods, everything looked the same, and after one hour driving all kinds of paths, I finally said to my wife that we had to block the roads which appeared to be a dead end with one of the many fallen trees that lay everywhere. So, every time we were on a dead-end and had to turn and go back and came at crossroads, I got out of the car and blocked that road with one of those trees. So, I'd know that it was no use to try that road ever again. Again, one hour later, we stumbled upon a couple of roads crossing. Luckily three of the roads appeared to be banned with trees! So, there was only one road open. So, that's the road we choose, and finally 30 minutes later, it turned out that this was the road which would lead us down into the valley. So, making failures is good, as long as you do something with it. Treat them as a dead-end sign and cross that road off to never visit again.

"Making failures can act as a dead-end sign to prevent you from doing the wrong things."

The further away your goal lies, and the more difficult your goal is, the more you will find yourself on dead-ends while trying to reach your goal. Dead-ends come in the form of all kinds of frustrations, interruptions, and distractions. The trick is to keep your end goal always in mind. This is why you want to make a Vision Board of your goal to motivate you to keep trying to find the right way to your goal. Develop the flexibility to find new ways as soon as you realize that you are on a dead-end.

That's the most significant advantage of making mistakes: they act as a Dead-End Sign and prevent you from wasting your time on doing the wrong things.

So, don't see making failures as a value judgment of your identity. No, it's only a sign that you have to try something else. Don't be a Don Quixote! Be an agile Kung Fu master who always finds his way to success. One of the things I like a lot about the Jason Bourne movies is that Jason Bourne always will find his way out to victory. No matter how desperate the situation seems where he has landed himself in, Jason Bourne has the confidence that he will always overcome every difficulty he encounters. That's because he is trained to see opportunities in almost every situation. If you are making a failure, don't freeze, and certainly don't try to cover it up! Think as Jason Bourne and ask yourself "Where is my opportunity to victory?!" Or as Maria Sharapova, one of the most successful women athletes of her time, has put it: "A 'No,' or a rejection, is just a sign that something better is coming."

To back this idea that making failures is the only way forward, I have a few quotes from the man who probably has made the most failures in his life: Thomas Edison. After 1,000 failures to invent the light bulb, he finally succeeded in creating the working light bulb. But his motto after each and every failure was always: "Yeah!! I have found yet another way not to proceed anymore. I have found another dead-end!"

So, here is just a glimpse of his enormous wisdom:

- Genius is one percent inspiration and ninety-nine percent perspiration.

- Our greatest weakness lies in giving up. The surest way to succeed is always to try just one more time.

- Many of life's failures are people who did not realize how close they were to success when they gave up.

- Opportunity is missed by most people because it is dressed in overalls and looks like work.

- There is no substitute for hard work.

- If we did all the things we are capable of, we would literally astound ourselves.

Anti-Procrastination Hack:

Start to see making mistakes as a way to quickly discover the dead-end signs on your way to your goal. The quicker you know that you are on a dead-end, the quicker you will find your way to your goal. So, start making mistakes as quickly as possible because it will make you more successful in achieving your goals!

Know, Understand and Acknowledge your Current Situation

We all have goals in our lives. Big goals and small goals. This means that we often are busy pursuing our goals. This is a way of thinking I'd like to call Results-thinking. More about that will be covered later in this book.

Develop an Anti-Procrastination Mindset

In my early twenties, I had a good and dear friend Roy. He was a couple of years older than me and played the trumpet in a Pop band he had organized himself. While I was playing the trombone, he asked me to join him in his group. I played for many years in his band, and we all had a great time. The band was playing very well, but just on an amateur level. But Roy had great dreams. He was always talking about international success and doing world tours and so on. He really believed that if we correctly played how it should be that we would be a highly successful renowned pop band. This sounds great, isn't it! I mean if you ever heard of positive thinking then here you have the guy who was thinking all the time positively! But, unfortunately for him, the band never got any success. Even not locally in our city. So, what happened? Why was his extreme kind of Results-thinking not bringing him the success he had hoped for? Well, that's because he totally forgot his current situation. He was not aware and did not understand and indeed was not acknowledging the fact the fact that he had an amateur band with unprofessional guys, like me, who just wanted to have a little bit of fun while playing music. His goal was so far-fetched from reality that it was quite impossible. You could argue that everything is possible with the right action. Well, that's true of course. But Roy didn't put in the proper effort because he was not aware of the unbridgeable gap he had to cross. But because of his unawareness of his current situation, he kept on believing that his goal was achievable. So, he kept on pursuing that purpose in the way he had done it before. With the same crappy result, of course. This is why it is essential to know your current situation well enough with regards to your goals so that you also understand the gap between your current situation and your goals and even acknowledge it. Ignoring the gap is no option, of course. Nor is whining and complaining.

For 25 years, I have worked as a Project Manager in large corporations, and in the hundreds of projects I have done, it was always concerned about making change happen. When I talked to my stakeholders about the project, they were almost always focusing only on the To-Be side of the equation. However, if you don't know where you stand now, how will you know where to go.

I always used this as an example. Let's assume that someone drops you in the middle of a forest. And your assignment is to go to the nearest village with the name "A." And, of course, you get a map of the territory. How will you know where to go? North? South? East? West? Well, if you don't know where you are right now relative to your goal, you don't know where to go. That's why it is essential to know your current situation. You not only need to know your current situation, but you also need to understand it and acknowledge it.

Let me give you an example. Let's say that your goal is to run the Marathon in New York next month. Okay great! Of course, you have done all kinds of positive visualization, so you have seen yourself pass the finish line a couple of times already. You will become more and more enthusiastic every time. You are highly motivated to run the marathon. But one day goes by and the next and the next. And suddenly you ask yourself why you haven't started preparing yourself. Well, the chances are that you have neglected your current situation. You are out of shape; you haven't run for months now. Your schedule with appointments the coming period is incredibly busy. So, you haven't explored your current situation with regards to your goal. So, where to start? Clean your agenda entirely for the next six weeks? Start running 16 hours per day? You don't know where to begin because you don't know where you are right now. No wonder that you are procrastinating!

So, the first thing you have to do is to examine your current situation with regards to your goal. What are the requirements to run the marathon of New York? You must be in shape. You must have the time to exercise and prepare. You must have the chance to attend the event. You must have the budget to travel and stay in New York. And so on and so on. Now given these requirements, what is your assessment of your current situation? Give yourself for each element a grade from 0 to 10. Zero means entirely not appropriate, ten means excellent qualification. Now, you know a couple of things. First of all, you can assess the viability of your goal. How SMART is your goal anyway? Secondly, you can determine your weakest link and make that your highest priority.

So, now you know your current situation. But do you fully understand it too? Do you know how big the gap is between your current situation and your wannabee situation? Have you done your negative visualization to find the obstacles on your way to your goal? Have you decided on how to attack those challenges?

Step 1: There is one place and one place only to depart from to your destination, and that is your current situation. So, you need to know where you are right now.

Step 2: Assess your current situation without judgment and check how you are doing with regards to the requirements of your goal. I mean, if you have been dropped in the forest and you don't know where to go to, so what your goal is, then why would you need to know where you are right now? See more on this in the chapter about developing your Results-thinking skills.

Step 3: Define the gap between your current situation and the necessary requirements.

So, now you know and understand your current situation? But do you acknowledge it too? If the current situation is not what you want, often people tend to ignore it or even fight against it. This is the worst you can do, of course, because it only brings you further from your goal. So, even if you have given yourself very low grades on the list of requirements, it still doesn't mean much. Don't judge it. It is like it is. And it is a reasonable assessment of where you are right now so that you know where to go from here. So, be glad that you did the evaluation, no matter how big the gap seems to be, between your current reality and your wished reality. Just see it as a stepping stone to make progress from there. Don't be an ostrich! Dare to look at your current situation in the most unbiased way possible. Only then you can start improving yourself in the direction of your goal.

Anti-Procrastination Hack:

Know, Understand and Acknowledge your Current Situation, so that you know for sure and with confidence what to do and where to start.

Develop an Anti-Procrastination Mindset

Develop Results-thinking skills to Motivate Yourself

This chapter focuses entirely on Results-thinking. This is one of the two components of The Anti-Procrastination Mindset. Always remember, that you need to balance Results-thinking with Process-thinking. You can read more on that in the next chapter. But for this chapter, the scope is only Results-thinking.

What is Results-thinking?

Do you like to be more successful and happy? Well, then here is the Ultimate Formula for Success:

The problem is that most people only look at the results side of the equation. They only see the success and happiness of other people and say "I want that too!" This is an extreme example of Results-thinking. Don't get me wrong! Results-thinking is good because it has the power to motivate you to do the hard work and overcome all obstacles and eventually achieve the level of success and happiness you aspire right now. But don't get lost in results-thinking only, like my friend Roy did (see Anti-Procrastination Hack #34). This will bring you nowhere.

Results-thinking is the way of thinking where you focus on the results side of the equation of the success formula. This is important, of course, because how else would you know which hard work needs to be done? This is your Mid-Term or Long-Term Vision, depending on the project or goal you are working on. The result is the tip of the iceberg. It is what you see other successful people succeed in. What you don't know, however, is what is below the surface of the water. What are all the elements which need to be done to see the result? This is why you also need to perform process-thinking.

Results-thinking gets and keeps you motivated

To let yourself be blinded by the tip of the iceberg, can also be positive. It provides you a huge strong drive and motivation that you can use to cover the heavy route to your goal. You don't know yet what it takes to reach your goal and which obstacles you will encounter along the way. So, having a strong motivation will help you to keep going until you have achieved your goal.

This is why many people have done things which were otherwise never done. Many projects would never have been started if you had known in advance what you would have encountered along the way to the achievement of your project.

Results-thinking is therefore also a strong motivator for you because otherwise, you would do nothing at all. And as always, it is about finding the right balance between Results-thinking and Process-thinking. So, limit your Results-thinking so that you will not be too optimistically. That will only get you disappointed and tempt you to give up. On the other hand, limit your process-thinking because otherwise, you will not start in the first place.

Results-thinking will **help you Start** what you want to Finish.

Process-thinking will **help you Finish** what you have Started.

To reap the benefits of Results-thinking, create a visual anchor. Often people use a Vision Board for that. Whatever your goal is, try to visualize the end-result into a colorful vision board. Place that vision board where you can see it daily so that you have a continuous conscious and subconscious reminder of your goals. This will help you motivate to persevere when the going gets tough.

Especially when you procrastinate because you are too obsessed with all the obstacles on your way, a vision board can help you to see through to the end.

Anti-Procrastination Hack:

Results-thinking done properly has the power to motivate you to achieve your goals until successful.

Don't become the exhausted centipede

If you focus entirely on Results-thinking, chances are that you are obsessed with all kinds of shiny objects you see. You start a new project every week, without finishing anything. If you are like that, you will never develop yourself further in one direction. So, after a month or a year, it appears that you have been very busy, but you have not achieved anything. You have not added any value to your life, your skills, and so on. You probably have not learned anything from it either.

To prevent this, you need to improve your decision-making process. Before you choose a new goal, you have to check whether you really want it or not. What is involved? Will you succeed?

Every new opportunity seems beautiful from the outside, but is this what you really want?

Sleep a few nights over it. Then the first shine is already gone, and you look at it a bit more down to earth. Your cold-thinking ability will have the chance to do its work.

Make a checklist for yourself. Before you pursue a new goal, you must have completed at least some steps. For example, step 1 is that you first create an overall picture of what the consequences are regarding time, money, effort, and so on. If, after that, your goal is still attractive enough, you might consider pursuing it. The chance that you will actually realize your goal will be much larger.

Results-thinking is also a way of strategic thinking about your goals and the way you will achieve them.

And thinking too much about that is also a way of procrastinating on actually doing the stuff you need to do. Every week or so, I invent a new way of working for myself. And every time I think that it will make me more productive, of course. And sometimes it helps me, sometimes it doesn't. But more often than not, it costs me too much time. Suddenly, I find myself busy with making new templates, spreadsheets, making Evernote notes, or what not. And before I know it, one or two hours are gone without me working on what I should do which is working on my goals.

Results-thinking gets you out of the flow of doing things. There is a psychological phenomenon called the centipede effect. This describes the effect which occurs when a normally automatic subconscious activity is disrupted by reflecting on it. The best description of this effect is, however, a poem by Katherine Craster:

> *A centipede was happy - quite! Until a toad for fun Said, "Pray, which leg moves after which?" This raised her doubts to such a pitch, She fell exhausted in the ditch Not knowing how to run.*

Flow is an optimal state of consciousness where everything seems to seamlessly and effortlessly while performing optimally. Flow is a state of consciousness where you feel at your best and where you perform at your best. These are the moments that you are so absorbed in what you are doing that everything else disappears. Your sense of self disappears, your sense of time disappears. According to a McKinsey study, it turns out that top executives in flow are five times more productive than the ones out of flow. So, if you want to stop procrastinating, then flow is where you want to be.

And this means that you need to stop your Results-thinking and start with Process-thinking. Please, don't become the exhausted centipede!

Anti-Procrastination Hack:

Results-thinking done inappropriately will cause that you either procrastinate or give-up on your goal entirely. You will lose the motivation to overcome the inevitable obstacles on your way to your goal.

It's Time to Develop your Passion

Your brain is continuously developing itself. Microscopic changes in individual neurons are continuously re-shaping your brain. But also larger changes appear in your brain such as cortical remapping in response to injury. Your brain of today is already different from that of yesterday. There is a fairly new science called neuroplasticity which is studying this. All these changes in your brain are caused by your behavior and environmental stimuli, but also by your thoughts and emotions. My point is, that if you want to, you could develop yourself into a totally different person within the next year. Your brain is really incredible in developing itself. So, whatever you like to pursue in your life, it is possible. However, for that to happen, you need a long-term focus of all your mental energy into that one direction. But what is that direction? That's where your Passion lies! So, start developing your Passion because it can work like rocket fuel for your brain to develop itself into the right direction and for you to be successful and happy.

To get rid of your procrastination, you must be aware that your mind is always able to change towards the direction you want. One of the drivers which can help you achieve this is your passion. Your passion is a kind of rocket energy you have inside you which drives you towards your goal.

For example, if you have a passion for painting, you think probably about it all day long. And when you come home in the evening, the first thing you will do is to paint for half an hour before you prepare your dinner. And after dinner, you will continue painting as soon as possible, because it is your passion. Are you going to delay that painting? No, of course not, because you have a huge internal drive.

It is not intelligence that separates successful people from the rest. It is also not skills or their parents. It is also not the amount of money they got from their parents. It is also not the network they had through their parents. No, it is nothing like that. The only thing which separates successful people from the rest is their passion. Because with that passion they were so hungry to develop themselves into the direction of their dreams, that they became unstoppable.

Ok, passion may sound like music in your ears, but have you already found your passion? And how do you develop your passion? Well, a great way to develop your passion is by creating a Vision Board.

Maybe you are thinking: "But I can't paint all day long! I have to do so many other things as well. And I don't want to postpone that either. But I also want to paint, so how do I deal with that?" It is possible also to develop a passion for doing boring tasks. Just think of the example of the stonecutter (p.217) who had developed a passion for helping build the cathedral. He is doing very dull work, but he is very passionate because he feels that he is building a cathedral. You can do this too by linking your tedious tasks to a higher purpose of yours, your passion. But the prerequisite for that is, of course, that you already have a passion.

Doing administration, accounting, keeping your house clean, these are all tasks that most people find annoying and that you would prefer to postpone, so that you can continue with your painting, for example. But what if you can fool yourself to believe that all these tasks contribute to your higher purpose to become an excellent painter, who earns full-time money with it? Then suddenly it becomes fun to do those tasks. Because at the moment that you are cleaning your house, you know that you are contributing to your professional painter career.

For example, my wife wants to become a yoga teacher for which she needs to follow a study of two years. But before she starts with that, she wants to have the house ready. So now she is busy with a lot of chores that are not fun, but it does make her feel like she is preparing her yoga training. And so, she is very motivated to do those chores. It may seem that she is cleaning up at that moment, or that she is redecorating the living room, but in reality, she is taking care of her higher goal. Isn't that a great way to develop your passion?

You need to become aware of the higher goals you have at this moment in your life. If you are choosing them well, you won't have more than five, because otherwise, it will be hard to focus on your higher purposes. With these five top goals, you can use a goals hierarchy as a kind of Christmas tree to relate all other goals and tasks to it. The next step is to develop a passion for your five higher goals. This is done by creating a very compelling visualization for each of them and making a Vision Board can help you a lot with that.

Anti-Procrastination Hack:

Develop a passion for your top five life purposes, so that you create rocket energy within you to relentlessly pursue your goals and so that even the most tedious tasks become enjoyable.

Eliminate every distraction which stands in the way of your Passion

Your passion is like an internal rocket engine that ignites you and propels you forward at rocket speed. The big question, however, is to where? Of course, you don't want to scatter as an unguided projectile, because then you just waste energy and that is a shame. You need to focus your rocket energy on what is important to you. And those are your most important values.

Values are at a very subconscious level the things that drive you every second of the day to do what you do. Those values are linked to a specific higher purpose. Every goal has its value hierarchy. So, first of all, you have to determine what your five most top goals are that you want to realize in your life. Let's assume that you can launch up to five rockets. Then, of course, you want to send them in the right directions. So, everything starts with determining your top five goals.

Focus your Passion with Laser-precision!

To determine your top five goals, follow the advice of one of the wealthiest and most successful men on earth, Warren Buffett.

Given his success, it stands to reason that Warren Buffett has an excellent understanding of how to spend his time wisely. Given his success, you could say that Buffet manages his time much better than anyone else.

If you eliminate the inessential things in your life, then you make your life easier. This is, in essence, a Lean Philosophy. As you learn in this book, every result is the consequence of a process of actions and decisions. If you want to stop procrastinating to become a highly effective and efficient goal-getter, you need to focus on optimizing this process. And according to the Lean philosophy, this is done by eliminating waste.

There are various types of waste which are frustrating your process to be successful. I will use the Lean terminology first and then explain what this has to do with your procrastination habit:

Passion Destroyer #1: Over-production

Over-production means that you perform tasks before they become necessary. For example, I like to develop my skills and learn new things. This means that I spend a fair amount of my time reading books, articles or following online courses. The big question is, however: is that time well spend? Well, to be honest: NO! Most of the time, I read and learn all these new things while they are not directly applicable in my life right now. Maybe, somewhere in the future, I can use this new knowledge. But, then it might need a refresh anyway. So, why bother now? Well, because it gives me a good reason to procrastinate on other things which need to be done right now. So, my challenge is to become a just-in-time learner! How about yours? What are the things you do right now while they are not necessary?

Anti-Procrastination Hack:

Make sure you don't perform activities which are not necessary right now because this might cause you to procrastinate on the things that are very important to do right now.

Passion Destroyer #2: Waiting

Waiting means that you can't continue pursuing your goal because you are dependent on some external factor which is not available for you right now. I have often had this in my life. When I finally set myself down to do the thing I was procrastinating on for so long, I very soon came to the conclusion that I missed one or more essential elements. This totally frustrated me, so that I became "idle" for the next few hours or so. Very inefficient, of course. So, prepare your activities with Process-thinking, so that you will be well prepared when you start your activity and don't have to wait for some essential input.

Anti-Procrastination Hack:

Use Process-thinking to prevent possible waiting times because this might cause you to procrastinate.

Passion Destroyer #3: Transport

Transport means that you have to move things unnecessarily. For example, if you want to train for the New York marathon every day, then you better make it a habit to have all your running gear in one place. Because if you need to search for your running shoes or shirt (or both!) tomorrow morning, the chances are that you'd rather want to procrastinate your training of that day until the next day. Again, this is where you need Process-thinking to help you organize your activities in such a way that unnecessary movement or transport is required.

Anti-Procrastination Hack:

Use Process-thinking to prevent unnecessary movement or transport of things which might tempt you to procrastinate.

Passion Destroyer #4: Over-processing

Over-processing means that you want to be perfect in what you do. Within the Project Management world, this is called "gold plating." You can also call it the 80-20 rule of success. In either way, it is unnecessary to put in 80% of the effort to get the quality of what you are working on from 80% to a 100% level. This is very inefficient and a good excuse for procrastinating. This is why you need Results-thinking to define what it means to accomplish your goal successfully. What are the requirements to make your goal worth an 8 on a 10-scale? If you want to run the New York marathon, for example, and your current personal record is to run a marathon in 4 hours and 30 minutes, what good does it do you to want to run the New York marathon in under 3 hours? This requires not only an awful lot of training and therefore time, but it is probably also the cause that you will procrastinate on running this marathon, or worse, that you will give up your goal entirely because you believe that it will never be possible. What a shame! Just set your goal to 4 hours and 25 minutes and run the damn marathon!

Anti-Procrastination Hack:

Use Results-thinking to avoid the trap of "gold plating your goal." Instead, make your goal realistic and achievable to avoid procrastinating on it.

Passion Destroyer #5: Inventory

Inventory means that you have unnecessary inventory in whatever shape or form. A great way to procrastinate I use a lot is to search Google for new hacks and shortcuts. For example, I need to write a new article on my website, and instead of just starting to write, I search Google for ideas on the topic. Most of the time, I end up one or two hours later, with a lot of interesting articles, but in the end not useful for my purpose. So, in the end, I still have to start writing my article. I would have been better off, starting to write this article immediately. This is why Process-thinking will help you to become a goal getter, instead of a procrastinator because it helps you to avoid this kind of distractions.

Anti-Procrastination Hack:

Use Process-thinking to avoid unnecessary distractions and instead make you unstoppable in achieving your goals.

Passion Destroyer #6: Defects

Defects means that the process of taking actions and decisions ends up with the wrong result. If you only run one mile each day, then it is hard to expect that you will be able to run a marathon in three months from now. This is why you need to balance Results-thinking with Process-thinking so that you can consistently evaluate if you are on the right track of achieving your goals, or not. If not, this will allow you to course correct effortlessly into the right direction. This will increase the chance that you will actually achieve your goals.

Anti-Procrastination Hack:

Balance Results-thinking with Process-thinking to continually course correct yourself on your way to achieving your goals.

Make Your Passion your most important Focus

To increase the chance of you realizing Your Passions, you need Focus!

Having Focus gives you the chance to eliminate all Passion Destroyers.

Focus helps you to determine your weakest link and do something about it.

Everything you do takes up your time, energy and maybe also your money. You better spend it wisely. And the best way to do that is to create focus in everything you do by choosing your top 5 Long-Term Goals wisely and by saying No to everything else.

This is why Warren Buffet uses this method to be highly successful:

Step 1: Draw up a list of the 25 most important goals you want to achieve in the next five to ten years.

Step 2: Choose from this list the five most important goals.

Step 3: Decide to only focus on these five goals from now on and to forget everything else.

Step 4: Use these top five goals to develop your passion for.

44

Anti-Procrastination Hack:

Every Passion deserves to be fulfilled, but this becomes only true if you focus your passion with laser-

> *precision. Use the 4-step process to decide on your top 5 goals for the coming years and say No to everything else.*

All tasks and activities you do from now on must be related to one of your five higher goals, so that everything you do is valuable and meaningful. In doing so, you reduce the chance of procrastination. Because things that you find valuable and meaningful, you will be very much likely to do. After all, you have a passion for it!

Furthermore, you will develop your passion for each higher purpose, so that each of your five missiles has enough rocket energy to reach your goal. You do this by creating a Vision Board per target with very bright images that make you very enthusiastic. You will also develop your Values around those objectives.

After that, you regularly have to pay attention, consciously and subconsciously, to your Vision Board and your Values. You can do this, for example, through your Vision Board, Future-Self Visualization and Positive Affirmations. That way you develop your Passion. And that Passion gives you a rocket that is focused on your target and flies off at rocket speed.

45

Anti-Procrastination Hack:

Develop a Passion for your top five life purposes, by using Vision Boards, Values, Future-Self Visualization, and Positive Affirmations.

Define your Long-Term Goals (aka Your Life's Mission)

Consciously thinking about your Long-Term Goals will give you a sense of Direction in your life. It will give your life more meaning and purpose. Furthermore, thinking about your Long-Term Goals will give you a broader perspective on your life. It will enable you to connect the dots. It gives you focus and enables you to stay focused.

Long-Term Goals give you more clarity on what you value and want the most. This will make you more determined by the choices you make every day. Moreover, Long-Term Goals will open up a sense of resourcefulness, so that you will be more receptive to opportunities, like new ideas, innovative thinking, tools, support systems, and so on.

Stephen Covey has written a book about Principle-centered leadership. He speaks about finding your "True North." If you have a True North in your life, then you have an internal compass you can always use in every situation. Developing, maintaining and working on your Long-Term Goals, is the best way to develop your True North. Whenever you get stuck in your life, you don't know what to do, or you feel lost, you will have your

True North in the form of your Long-Term Goals to guide you through that period of uncertainty.

So, if you want more control over your life, now is the time to set your goals in life. It will channel all your energy towards your True North. It will make you more responsible, more in control and more powerful. And when setting Long-Term Goals, don't limit yourself. Instead, follow your wildest dreams and go even beyond that. Become the best possible version of yourself!

To set your goals adequately, the only thing you have to do is to make sure that your goals are clear. If you have a fuzzy goal, then it is like walking into a fog. I assume that you want to walk into a bright and shiny future, so set clear goals. This means that you have to be very specific: what will you see, what will you hear, what will you feel, what will you taste, what will you smell and what will you say to yourself when you have achieved your goal? If you can answer these questions, then your goal is clearly defined.

Furthermore, your goals need to have a deadline. A goal without a deadline is just a dream. So, for every Long-Term Goal you set, make sure to put a deadline on it. This will also encourage you to work on your Long-Term Goals frequently.

Your goals need to be measurable because how would you otherwise know that you have accomplished them?

46

Anti-Procrastination Hack:

Set your goals adequately so that you have the maximum chance of success. Your Long-Term Goals serve as your True North, and you don't

> *want to throw away your energy and resources by driving yourself in the wrong direction. So, make sure your goals are challenging, clear and well-defined, have a deadline and are measurable.*

The 5-step process for defining your Long-Term Goals

There is a process which increases the chance for you to achieve your Long-Term Goals. This process consists of the following steps:

Step 1: Choose an area in your life for which you want to set your Long-Term Goals for.

Step 2: Brainstorm about your goals in the chosen life area.

Step 3: Choose the top 1 goal in the chosen life area.

Step 4: Make your goals SMART.

Step 5: Write your goals down and give them a visual representation.

Repeat this process (steps 1 to 5) for all areas of your life to make sure you have covered every area of your life.

I will now describe in detail what the best practices are for each of the 5 steps:

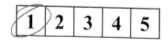

Step 1: Choose an area in your life for which you want to set goals for:

I assume that you are a person who wants to balance his life. With balancing I mean not only work/life balance, but also life/life balance. You play multiple roles in your life, and you play on different chess boards simultaneously. You are maybe a father or a mother of your kids, so you want to spend time with them and also have goals with them and for them. You are a husband or wife, and you also want to bring time together with your spouse. And also in that area you probably have goals. You are playing sports and have goals in that area. And so on.

So, instead of only setting goals for your career, for example, you also need to think about your other life areas. And don't forget about yourself! Probably you also have some personal development goals.

Let's have a closer look at the different life areas:

Personal Development Goals

Whatever you do in your life, you will always bring yourself with you. So, if you would become the best version of yourself, then everything you do will improve tremendously. So, when setting goals in life also think about setting goals for your personal development. They may fall into one of the following categories:

- **Physical goals:** these are goals related to how you look and feel physically, such as fitness goals, health goals, goals related to appearance or lifestyle.

- **Emotional goals:** these are goals related to how you feel and how you will react to all kinds of circumstances. Think about becoming more stable and happier.

- **Mental goals:** these are goals related to better thinking, gaining more focus, developing your intelligence and peace of mind.

- **Spiritual goals:** these are goals related to the non-physical aspects of your life. It might be that you want to have a deeper connection with the world around you or that you want to develop a calm mind.

Family and Relationship Goals

Family and relationships are also a main and very important area of your life worth setting goals for. You can set goals to improve current relationships, abandon relationships and develop new relationships. It's up to you to choose what you want. But you better choose consciously now, instead of "letting it all happen." But whatever goal you set, be specific. So, for example, say that you want to call your best friend every week from now on. Or maybe you want to take your spouse on a date every month. Or you want to attend a networking event every two weeks.

Career Goals

If you are like me, then your career is where you spent the most of your hours awake every week, so this is a major part of your life. What are your goals regarding your career? Where do you want to be next year? And where do you want to be in five years from now? And where do you want to be when you are 60 or 70 years old? Do you want to stay the rest of your life in the career you have now? Or do you want to deepen that or broaden that? And do you want to stay in a job or rather start your own company? And what type of clients do you prefer to work with?

Financial Goals

You will have income from your career. But maybe you want also to generate a passive income stream? How will you do that? By making some investments? And what about your costs? What goals do you have in that area? Do you want to save enough money for early retirement? Do you want to leave your kids with a trust fund?

Community Goals

When we are young, we are taking much from the community we live in. Education is such an example. Or moral and financial support from the people around us. But there comes a time that you will want to give back to your community. Maybe you even want to leave a legacy after you are gone? So, what are your goals in this area? Will you start a charity fund? Will you give children in your neighborhood extra mentor lessons? Will you volunteer at a school? Giving can fulfill you with great joy. So, why would you withhold yourself from that pleasure?

Anti-Procrastination Hack:

The first step towards crafting your Long-Term Goals for your life is to choose an area in your life for which you want to develop your goals for.

Step 2: Brainstorm about your goals in the chosen life area:

Now think of the area in your life you have chosen to develop your goals for (the outcome of step1). For example, let's say that you have chosen to develop Long-Term Goals for the area of Community goals. Inside this area, what would your perfect life look like in a few years from now?

And in 10, 20, 30, 40 years from now?

What type of role would you prefer to have?

How would you like to interact?

Write down your first brainstorm of goals in the chosen area.

I suggest to let your list mature for a couple of days in the back of your head. Then after a couple of days, review your list and see if you have any new ideas on what your Long-Term Goals for this particular life area might look like. Then after you have completed your list, go on to the next step.

Anti-Procrastination Hack:

The second step towards crafting your Long-Term Goals for your life is to brainstorm goals within a chosen life area.

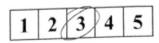

Step 3: Choose the top 1 goal in the chosen life area:

After you have created a list of goals you'd like to achieve in the chosen life area, now choose the top 5 goals. First, prioritize all the goals. Put the most important goal on top, then the second most important goal, and so on. The least important goal will obviously at the end of your list.

Now, you see what your top 5 goals are on your list. Again, let this mature in the back of your head for a couple of days and then come back to it. Is your top 5 still the top 5 most important Long-Term Goals?

49

Anti-Procrastination Hack:

The third step towards crafting your Long-Term Goals for your life is to choose the top 5 goals per life area.

[INTERMEDIATE STEP]

Now, repeat step 1 to 3 for all your five life areas. After that you probably have 5 times 5 equals 25 Long-Term Goals, covering all areas of your life. How's that for a balanced life!!

Now, comes the hard and scary part!!

Prioritize all 25 goals. The most important goal comes on top, and the least important goal comes at the end of your list. Again, let the list mature for a couple of days. Then review the list again and check if the list is still prioritized in the way you want it to be.

Now, consciously choose to only work on your top 5 goals until you have fully achieved them. And decide to throw away and forget all the other goals and never come back to them until you have accomplished your top 5 goals. This is exactly how Warren Buffet became the multi-billion-dollar man he is today.

Or, as Confucius wisely said:

> *"The man who chases two rabbits catches neither."*

Don't take the risk of spoiling your rocket energy chasing too many stars. Focus on just your top 5 goals!!!

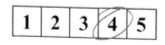

Step 4: Make your top 5 goals SMART:

While you have now decided on your top 5 goals you want to accomplish the coming years, it is time to define these goals in a way that chances of you achieving this goal are maximal. In other words, you need to make sure that your goal is defined in a SMART way. It means that your goal needs to be Specific, Measurable, Acceptable, Realistic and Time-framed.

So, check if your goals are **specific enough**. What will you see, what will you hear, what will you feel, what will you taste, what will you smell and what will you say to yourself when you have achieved your goal? If you can answer these questions, then you know that your goal is described specific enough.

Check if your goal is **measurable**, how else would you know that you have achieved your goal?

And your goal must be **acceptable**. This means that your goals must be good for you, for the people around you and ultimately for the whole planet.

Make also sure that your goal is **realistic**. Yes, it may be a big and challenging goal, but you must at least have a chance to realize it.

Finally, check if your goal has a **deadline**.

Anti-Procrastination Hack:

Make sure that your Long-Term Goals for your life are well-defined and SMART.

Step 5: Write your Long-Term Goals down and give them a Visual Representation:

Now, that you have crafted your challenging and SMART goals, it is time to write them down on your life's mission list.

Create for each of your five Long-Term Goals a separate Vision Board on which you give your goal a visual representation. Your life's mission is not something you want to treat lightheartedly. This is serious business!

Anti-Procrastination Hack:

Write your Long-Term Goals down and give them a visual representation.

The Dead-End versus Obstacle Paradox

What if one of your top 5 Long-Term Goals appear to be not feasible?

When I was a teenager, I played the trumpet as a hobby. But I was so enthusiastic that it became my dream to become a professional trumpet player. For that, I had to attend the Conservatory. One day, when I was still studying the trumpet at our local City Music School, I was summoned to go to the Dean of the school. Very carefully he explained to me that although I was a great amateur trumpet player, I would never be able to get to the professional level I was dreaming about. The specific bone structure of my mouth and the way my lips were built, would never allow me to play in the high register like professionals ought to do. Of course, I was devastated for a while. My dream I had for a very long time was utterly broken. After a while, I decided to refocus myself. I changed instruments, from trumpet to trombone, and I decided to only play on an amateur level and to pursue a career in something else. So, I also focused more on my study at High School, so that I would be able to attend University afterward. Shit happens in life, and sometimes a goal appears to be not feasible.

Life is unpredictable. So, how can you predict if your Long-Term Goal will be feasible in the end? Most of the time, it takes time to discover the feasibility. And by the time, you have found that a particular goal is not feasible, then don't keep on pursuing it, like a Don Quixote, or like my friend Roy did, of whom I told you earlier about. Decide on your plan B. So, delete this particular goal from your list of Long-Term Goals. This frees up mental energy for another Long-Term Goal which you can then add to your top 5 Long-Term Goals List. This will also change your goals hierarchy and values hierarchy.

Of course, you need to give yourself a chance in achieving your Long-Term Goals. It is no use to think already after a couple of days, weeks or months that your Long-Term Goal is not feasible. When I was eight years old, I started playing the piano, and although I didn't like it, I didn't give up quickly, because as my father always said, you need to pull through the hard beginning. Every beginning is hard, but don't let that scare you away from going forward. Eventually, it will go smoother, and if you then still don't like to pursue it, then you have a good reason to end the journey. Like I did, when I was 14 years old and decided to stop actively practicing the piano and changed towards the trumpet.

Anti-Procrastination Hack:

There is a fine line between giving up too quickly and chasing your dreams too long. The art of life is to balance that fine line in your advantage. You don't want to be a Don Quixote, but you also don't want to be a loser who never achieves anything. This is why you need to balance your Results-thinking with Process-thinking. This will give you a higher chance of making wise decisions to your advantage.

So, how do you know if you are on a dead-end or that you just have to deal with an obstacle? How do you know that you have to stay in line, like the stonecutter in the picture I have shown you earlier, and just overcome the last obstacle standing between you and your goal as opposed to giving up the idea of achieving your goal because it is simply not feasible?

Was Thomas Edison after 900 failures to invent the light bulb on a dead-end? Or was it just another obstacle he had to overcome? Well, history has taught us that it was an obstacle because after yet another 100 tries he finally succeeded. So, in hindsight, it was yet another obstacle. But what if he would have seen it as a dead-end? Then he would have stopped his journey to invent the light bulb. And then probably someone else would have invented it sometime later. It is tough to have this insight when you are in the middle of the process. That's why Process-thinking alone will not help you succeed. But when you also apply Results-thinking you give yourself an eye on the big picture and then it is easier to see what is happening. Results-thinking will provide you with a helicopter view and also a motivation to see things through to completion. Get in line and stay in line!

Was my friend Roy only dealing with obstacles instead of being on a dead-end? Well, unfortunately, he was not coping with obstacles at all because he had no realistic view of his current reality. He only performed Results-thinking without Process-thinking. That's why he kept chasing a wild dream without making any progress.

So, if you are stuck, you have to evaluate if you are on a dead-end rather than dealing with obstacles. One of the questions to ask yourself to make this evaluation is whether you have dealt with obstacles effectively and enough. Are you only at 40% of your reserve tank or have you given everything you have to find that it is impossible to overcome the obstacles?

Use both Results-thinking and Process-thinking to help you answer this question. And after that, take a wise decision to either end the project or pursue with it and deal with the obstacles effectively.

Anti-Procrastination Hack:

Use both Results-thinking and Process-thinking to get unstuck. Evaluate if you have dealt with obstacles effectively and efficiently and decide on ending the project you are working on or pursuing with it and dealing with the challenges. Either way, take a conscious decision.

How to perform Results-thinking?

With Results-thinking, the aim is to focus on one Long-Term Goal at once. Long-Term can be a couple of weeks, months, or even years. That's depending on the scope of the goal you are working on. For example, if you have to relocate to another state within three months from now, then a long-term view of your goal means a period of three months. But if you want to change careers for which you also need to get some certifications, then a long-term view is a couple of years. While a couple of years is too abstract for most human beings to get a grip of, you have to break that super long-term view down in several long-term views of one year, as you will learn below.

Step 1: Define the Scope of your Results-thinking process

If you are Results-thinking, choose what the scope of your thinking will be. It will probably be a Mid- or Long-Term Goal you want to achieve. Let's call this goal "X."

Step 2: With regards to the chosen scope "X," ask yourself the following questions:

- What will be accomplished when X is finished? Describe this in specific terms. Try to make it visual. So, instead of saying "I want to run long-distances" you say "I want to run the New York marathon next year." And you can create a visual of New York, the marathon and you in it.

- What are the positive outcomes when I have accomplished X?

- What are the negative outcomes when I have accomplished X?

- What will be the impact of accomplishing X for myself, my family, friends, stakeholders, and eventually the world?

- What will be the positive outcomes when I do not accomplish X?

- What will be the negative outcomes when I do not accomplish X?

- What are the possible obstacles on my way to accomplishing X?

- Use Negative Visualization to brainstorm all possible things that can go wrong with X.

- What can I do to prevent the obstacles from happening?

- If, in any case, an obstacle will happen, what will be my most adequate response to deal with the obstacle effectively?

- Define the requirements necessary to achieve X.

- Assess your current situation with regards to the requirements for X.

- Define the gap between your current situation and the achievement of X.

- Define for every 4-week period what the milestones are you need to have accomplished to achieve your end goal X.

Asking yourself this type of questions upfront will help you to be well-prepared to accomplish X, and it will set you up for successful achievement of X without having to procrastinate on it or to give up on it.

54

Anti-Procrastination Hack:

To perform Results-thinking, use this two-step process:

1) Define the scope of your thinking;

2) Ask yourself the different questions within the chosen scope.

Define your quarterly goals

By now, you should have defined the five Long-Term Goals you want to achieve in the coming years. So, for example, for your career field, you have determined where you want to grow in the coming years. This is a Long-Term Goal that needs to be made concrete using concrete milestones. At a certain moment, you have to switch from Results-thinking to Process-thinking, but that is too difficult if your Long-Term Goal is too abstract. Therefore, you want to define Medium-Term or Quarterly Goals that are defined more concretely. Based on these goals, it is easier to determine concrete actions for the coming week and to apply Process-thinking.

For example, suppose your Long-Term Goal is to switch to a completely different profession. You may need some training certificates for this new profession which you don't have right now. Preferably you also have some experience in that direction; in the new professional sector in which you want to work

Wanting to achieve all of that in a few years is one thing, but what do you have to do first?

To find out, it is a best practice to break-up your very big goal in some concrete milestones which you can realize in periods of 3 months.

In other words:

- Create quarterly goals, and

- Create an evaluation moment every 3 months where you can evaluate whether you are still on the right track or not.

- Is everything still going according to plan?

- Have you realized the milestones for these three months?

Quarterly goals are also an easy way to plan your next quarter so that you know what needs to be done within the next three months. What are the big milestones that have to be ready in three months from now and how are you going to realize that?

Break-down your Long-Term Goal in periods of 3 months. Ask yourself what you need to have realized in every quarter. This is obviously not a mathematical calculation. The point is that you know in general terms what you have to plan next quarter to achieve your Long-Term Goal in about three years from now. It's important to evaluate your progress every three months so that you know if your Long-Term Goals will still be feasible.

Organize a strategy session with yourself every three months where you evaluate your top 5 Long-Term Goals.

Take a look at what you have accomplished over the past three months to achieve those goals. Did you achieve all the milestones? If not, why not? If so, why? Could you have done it faster? Should you have chosen a slightly different direction?

Next, you will determine the impact of the results of the last three months are for all the other planned milestones. Maybe you need to do some adjusting to one or more milestones to make sure that your Long-Term Goal stays feasible.

Your quarterly goals are the bridge between Results-thinking and Process-thinking.

After you have evaluated the past quarter, it is time to plan your next. Which milestones need to be finished next quarter? Remember, goals, as well as milestones, need to be defined in a SMART way. So, for every quarterly goal, make sure that it is defined SMART. This makes it easier to start Process-thinking on a day-to-day basis for your quarterly goals. Use the questions in step 2 of the Results-thinking Process to help you with this.

The final result of drawing up your quarterly goals is a sheet of paper for every Long-Term Goal. On every sheet of paper, you will have well-defined and SMART quarterly goals per Long-Term Goal.

Use this sheet of paper every day when you are doing Process-thinking, where you ask yourself what the actions are that you have to carry out in the coming days so that the goal in question will be realized in three months.

Hopefully, you already have a Vision Board for your Long-Term Goals by now. It is also a good practice to make a Vision Board for your quarterly goals. Your quarterly goals are much more concrete than your Long-Term Goals, of course. And if you visualize them you can re-program your mental filters. This makes you much more alert and open to actual occurrences related to your goals. You will start to see more chances and opportunities, and you will become more flexible and resilient in dealing with obstacles.

Anti-Procrastination Hack:

Define quarterly goals as a bridge between Results-thinking and Process-thinking to help you actually get results and stay on track.

Develop your Burning Internal Motivation

A key secret to controlling your procrastination temptation is to develop a Burning Internal Motivation (BIM). If you are a car, then your BIM is your all-in-one starting engine and motor engine. You need your BIM to get started and to get going even when the going gets tough. So, if you really want to procrastinate less, start developing your BIM!

If you are like me, then you have probably seen a lot of time management tasks and to-do apps. I must say that I have tried a lot. I invested a lot of time in filling those apps with all kind of to do's. Every new app has at least cost me a couple of hours if not days to set it up. I must admit, that this is a great way of procrastinating on the real tasks while you have the illusion that you are busy! And a couple days, sometimes weeks and a lot of frustration later, I always decided to get rid of those apps or methods. Why? Because it doesn't work for me. There is something funny going on. The more I have scheduled for my to-do list, the less I get done. And the tasks on my to-do list, I always ignore. This makes me feel guilty and makes me even less productive. The more I have on my to-do list, the more I tend to procrastinate on it.

How about you? Do you recognize yourself in my story? If so, please read on:

Anti-Procrastination Hack:

Procrastination is a good thing as long as it concerns tasks which are not on your top 5 of priorities!

Lead Yourself in the right Direction

One of the reasons that you procrastinate, as we have seen earlier, is that you fear the unknown. So, to stop procrastinating, you need to get comfortable with the unknown. Later in this book, you will learn how to tap into your reserve tank and get used to feeling uncomfortable (the real key to willpower). In this chapter, I am going to show you a really cool way to get already yourself acquainted with the unknown. Dreaming about areas in your life you want to explore and dreaming about future accomplishments is a great way to explore the unknown already and get acquainted with it so that when the time arrives, you will be more comfortable with the new situation already. Moreover, you will be eager to start exploring it without procrastinating on it. The way to do this is by creating a compelling Vision Board for yourself. Here is how:

Develop your Vision Board to give you Direction of your life

Vision boards can help you create great results in your life. That is if you use the vision board and the vision board ideas correctly. Making your dream board can be a great inspiration to help you stay focused on your goals. Vision boards are used by almost all successful people because of the motivating and focusing power vision boards have. So, start using your vision board ideas today and read on for the tips:

Maybe you are asking right now what is a vision board, so let's that answer first. A dream board is a collage of images, pictures, symbols and ideas that will inspire you to pursue your goals and dreams. Vision boards are also called dream boards because they give you the chance of dreaming of your future. But a vision board serves much more purposes than just dreaming about the future, as you will find out when you read further.

As said, a vision board is an inspirational collage. The dream board you make will be a visual representation of your future. A tangible representation or idea of where you are going. Vision boards represent your ideal life, your dreams, and your goals. Making a dream board is a fun way to work on establishing a vision for your future. This vision may be a particular event in your near future or a more general direction you want to take the next few years. A vision board will give you the clarity about where your life is heading to. Instead of living day by day you now have a point on the horizon which will be your beacon.

"Your brain is like a holographic projector. It's your choice which slides you use to project your life into the world."

You know what they say about pictures, don't you? A picture can say more than a thousand words. That's why your brain loves pictures. In fact, pictures are the language of your subconscious mind.

As we have seen in chapter 3, the reptilian brain only understands visual images while the optic nerve is directly connected to your reptilian brain. That's why visualization techniques work so well because this is the best way to influence your reptilian brain. And your reptilian brain determines where your conscious mind and subconscious mind will pay attention to or not.

And your subconscious mind, if you like it or not, is steering your life. Did you know that most decisions are based on emotions rather than logic? So, if you can steer your subconscious mind in the right direction then you automatically will take decisions which will bring you nearer your goals. Sounds great, doesn't it?

Furthermore, you automatically will help all your subconscious powers to be aligned with the right direction. How often have you experienced that you said to work out more or eat healthier but then very quickly gave up? This inconsistent behavior is caused by the fact that a variety of your subconscious powers had other plans with you. All to protect you, of course. But what if your subconscious mind will be set for 100% driving you towards your goals? That would make you extremely successful!

It is like a carriage with eight horses. The most efficient way is when all horses are running in precisely the same direction, fully aligned with each other and with the coachman, who determines the direction. That's why it is important to determine your Long-Term Goals first, and after that making them tangible with a vision board. Creating a vision board and using your vision board consistently will program your subconscious mind in the right way.

Most people use a vision board in a place where they will often see it. A vision board consists mainly of pictures, but you can also add some keywords that represent your dreams and goals. By placing your vision board in a place where you will often see it, you will be able to start visualizing on it better and better. Frequently visualizing your goals and dreams is a requirement for your subconscious mind to be reprogrammed towards your goals.

A vision board is easy to share with the important people around you. For every goal, you have you need support. And the best way to organize and get that support is to involve your important people in your dreams, goals, and plans as early as possible.

Use your vision board for goal-setting

To be successful and achieve your goals, you must at least have your goals top of mind. One way is to write your goals down at least once every day, but another way is to create a visual representation of your goals by making a vision board. This will inspire you to seek ways to get closer to your goals continuously. If you picture your ideal life on a vision board and place your vision board on a prominent place in your house, then you will consciously and subconsciously see your ideal life a couple of times each day!

This is one of the ways you can use visualization to train your brain to get accustomed to your new situation. Visualization is the language of your subconscious mind. To activate your subconscious mind, you have to visualize goals. It is not enough to say "I want to lose ten pounds." That's not something your subconscious mind can process. But if you see an image of yourself being ten pounds' slimmer, then your subconscious mind will understand the message. Your subconscious mind will let you see new opportunities you have never seen before, and it will ignore distractions which will withhold you from putting in the effort necessary to get slimmer.

So, practice visualization each day. Make it a daily habit. You will become much more motivated to work on your goals. You will see that your vision board will fire up your internal motivation and notice that you will unexpectedly do something different than you are accustomed to. Suddenly you find yourself speaking out at meetings, taking more responsibility, taking more risks and experiencing bigger pay-offs.

Every goal has a multitude of factors which are important to understand and notice. But we as human beings have an insufficient thinking capacity. I don't say that you are dumb, I only say that we can only focus on seven plus or minus two things at the same time. That's why a vision board works perfectly for goal-setting because it gives you a chance to work on your goals and vision multiple times. Each time your vision will improve, and your goal-setting will improve. They will become more tangible every time, and exactly that is what your subconscious mind needs.

Furthermore, a vision board will give you the chance to get feedback from people around you which often will lead to new insights with which you can refine your vision and goal-setting.

Anti-Procrastination Hack:

Use your Vision Board to improve your goal-setting and to help you visualize your goals.

How to make a vision board that is compelling and motivating?

One of the big questions you should ask yourself is how you want to feel. If you had a magic wand and you could choose everything, answer this question: *How do I want to feel in my ideal life?*

Now, find pictures, images, symbols that represent that feeling. Of course, this might also be multiple feelings. When working on your vision board, you will soon find out that it is impossible to represent "I want not to feel anxious anymore" with an image. This is important to understand. Your subconscious mind cannot process negatives. So, as soon as you start to think about not being anxious then your subconscious mind will immediately create an image of anxiety.

You don't want this!

So, focus only on positive feelings that you really want! And then find similar pictures, photos, images, symbols and colors for your vision board. To fill your vision board, you can use images from magazines or print pictures you find online, or you can draw pictures yourself. It is up to you! There is no right or wrong in making a dream board. As long as it represents your vision of your future, then it doesn't matter how you do it.

A vision board is an excellent way to work together with multiple people in forming a joint vision of a project for the near future. This might be with your family to plan your next big holiday. Or you can make a vision board together with your colleagues at work to develop a joint vision of where the department should evolve to the next year.

Types of Vision Boards

Here is something important. Let's say that you make a vision board with your spouse and kids to visualize your next holiday trip. You all have done a great job, and the result is astonishing! A very compelling vision board has been created! But hey, what do I see? On the vision board are two images with regards to your ideal career. Also, compelling but out of context. What does this do with the overall power of your holiday vision board you think? Exactly! The power of your vision board diminishes when it gets mixed with other not relevant images.

So, decide before you start what the context of your vision board will be.

What type of vision board are you going to make?

- A Project Vision Board for a well-defined project like your next holiday or a professional project you are working on?

- A Long-term Life Design Vision Board picturing your ideal future life in 5-10 years' time?

- A Life-area Vision Board picturing your ideal life in a particular area like your health or your education?

- A Long-Term Goal Vision Board visualizing how realizing your Long-Term Goal will look like?

A picture may say more than a thousand words, but only if it is the right image. So, when selecting the images for your vision board, first define as concrete as possible how you want to feel. Then start looking for similar pictures. After having selected twenty or thirty pictures, ask yourself which best represent your ideal feeling. Then only select a few pictures. Fewer is better in this case, especially when you have selected the best pictures.

Vision Board recipe (9 steps) for an exciting life

Here is my recipe for making a vision board that empowers and motivates you.

Nine steps in three phases:

- Preparation phase
- Creation phase
- Manifestation phase

Vision Board Preparation phase

Step 1: Select a category or context in which you want to create your vision board.

Please, re-read the above paragraph about choosing the right context for your Vision Board. It is important to be very clear about the context for your Vision Board, so choose for which Long-Term Goal you want to make your Vision Board.

Step 2: Make sure that within the chosen context (step 1) that the goal you want to make a Vision Board for, is defined SMART

You cannot visualize your goals if you don't know them, so this is a significant step. If you have chosen your goal you want to make a vision board for, describe it first in concrete terms, remember, we talked about this earlier in this book. This will make it easier to select corresponding pictures in the next step.

The more narrowed down you choose your context, the more powerful your vision board will be for you. Think of a laser who bundles all its energy just on one point. This extreme focus makes the laser unstoppable. So, choose with Laser Power!

Step 3: Collect a bundle of magazines with beautiful pictures.

This can be a magazine you can use to cut out pictures. Personally, I also cut out pictures from books I own if I find the pictures compelling enough, but okay, that's just me. Another source is the internet. Just search on Google for a term describing your goal. See step 2 for words in your goal description you can use. Then click search and go to the tab Images. Here you find a wealth of images you can choose from for your vision board. Download the image, print it out in full color and put it on your vision board.

Step 4: Select the images that represent your goals.

Take some time to go through all the magazines you have and search the internet. Make the first selection of 20 to 30 images. Look for the images which immediately inspire and excite you. Remember that the images must resemble your most optimal feeling.

Step 5: Wait a few days and then make the final selection of the images you want to use for your vision board.

Take the first selection of 20 to 30 images you created in step 4 and narrow them down the best 8 to 10. Go through the images one by one, and only select the images which give you the best feeling.

Vision Board creation phase

Step 6: Start making your vision board by adding picture by picture to your vision board.

Just buy a large piece of construction or poster paper. Then glue or tape your pictures to the paper. Choose an arrangement of the pictures that most pleases you. Write the creation date on your vision board. This gives you in future times when you look back some perspective on the journey you have already gone in life.

Step 7: Add some motivational quotes or words that best describe your optimal feeling.

These words represent your core values of your future life. It will be words like powerful, successful, abundance, fearless, pleasure, strong, joy and so on. Think of your desired future with regards to your chosen goal and decide what your core values should be and write them on your vision board.

You also might want to add some numbers if they have enough power to you. When I was working for a large Telecommunications company in The Netherlands, the Vision of our CEO for the next fiscal year was summed up in three numbers: 1 – 3 – 1,000. As you can see in the picture below, these three numbers became quite "a big thing" in the company:

They stood for:

- 1 Team: while the company was restructured, it was an important strategic goal to melt the various parts into one team again;
- 3 Customer Life Cycles;
- 1,000 Business Improvements in the next fiscal year.

This is a great example of how you can visualize even something very abstract as strategic goals for a large company.

Vision Board manifestation phase

Step 8: While you have created your vision board, it is the time that you start to manifest your vision board.

Take a few moments to contemplate on your vision board every day. Place your vision board in a place where you will see it a couple of times every day. Make it a daily habit to consciously watch your vision board. Even better would be if you would watch your vision board twice a day: just after you've got up in the morning and just before you go to bed at night. When watching your vision board say a few positive affirmations to yourself which confirm your goals. And if you watch your vision board at the end of the day, evaluate the events of that day as a living proof of you manifesting your dream board.

A vision board helps you to remind you every day of what is important to you. It will make it easier for you to take the right decisions. Better decisions will lead to better results. A vision board will also give you the chance to evaluate your decisions and actions on a day to day basis and learn from it.

Your vision board will also become your beacon in times that you have lost faith in yourself or your goals (or both). Looking and studying your vision board in your daily routine will then give you extra inspiration to push through tough times. Don't give up on your goals and dreams! Instead, use your vision board to guide you through dark times.

Step 9: After some time, your vision board might need an update.

See it as a 2.0 or 3.0 version of your vision board. Dependent from situation to situation, this might be after a couple of months or maybe after a year. But somewhere in the future, you will find that your vision board is not as compelling as it was. Most of the time this is because you have already achieved one or more of the goals, but it might also be that your life has evolved and took another turn, and the goals on the vision board are maybe not fulfilled completely, but they are also not valid anymore. Then you know that it is time to either update your vision board or make a completely new one.

Anti-Procrastination Hack:

Create your Vision Board in three phases: Preparation, Creation, and Manifestation to focus your mental energy and become a goal getter instead of a procrastinator.

Vision Board examples

To give you a feeling of how vision boards can look like I give you two vision board examples of my personal life. Every vision board is strictly personal, of course, so my vision board is only to give you an illustration, nothing more than that.

The first vision board example I made 15 years ago in what now seems like another life:

As you can see, I collected pictures from magazines and some of my photographs.

Here is another example I made for a project I was working on, but this time I made the vision board on my computer and printed it out later:

59

Anti-Procrastination Hack:

Vision Boards are a powerful tool for you to gain focus and motivation to work on your short-term and Long-Term Goals. Your Vision Board will help you stay focused and motivated even when distractions and setbacks arise on your way to your goal (which is a fact of life). Let your Vision Board end your procrastination temptation!

Motivate Yourself every step of the way

Whether you believe it or not, there is only one thing that motivates you every second of the day to do what you do. Not only that, but it also is the one thing that will make you happy or not when you evaluate how things have worked out for you. Would you like to know what this one thing is? It's your Values!

Your Values are the things that matter most to you. They determine your priorities on a deep subconscious level. Most of the time you are not consciously aware of your values. However, they drive you to do what you do all the time. Values are what you believe is most important to you in the way you live and work. Values are also the measures you use to tell if your life is turning out how you want it to be, or not. If you are behaving in line with your values, you are the happiest person on the planet. But if you don't align with your values, something feels wrong, and this can result in unhappiness or frustration. So, if you want to be happier and more successful in your life, then please take the time to get to know your values.

Knowing your personal values will make you Happy, Successful, Decisive, and a Goal Getter. No more Procrastination!

Why it is important to know your Personal Values

Knowing your values can make your life a lot easier. If you know your personal values, it will be easier for you make decisions which are in line with your core values. And when your decisions are in line with your core values you will be more consistent over time and more persistent. Remember that one of the causes of your procrastination temptation is two types of inconsistency: Internal Friction and Time Inconsistency.

I saw an interview with Tom Cruise way back in 2005 when he was dating Katie Holmes. He was asked how it felt to be in love. "It gives me inner peace," he answered. I can relate to that because I felt the same when I married my wife, Deborah. In all the years before I was always looking at girls and weighing my chances. I had closed this phase in my life which gave me inner peace.

The same applies when you act according to your core values. It gives you inner peace because you know that you don't have to look elsewhere anymore. You can quickly decide to stick to your own personal values which make you consistent over time. Furthermore, you will be more centered because your behavior is aligned with your values. You won't have questions like this anymore:

- What type of job should I pursue?

- Should I accept this new job opportunity or not?

- Or should I start my own business?

- Should I be firm, or should I compromise on my position?

- Should I travel down a new path or should I follow tradition?
- Should I start next activity or not?

These types of uncertainty are history when you know your core values. You will have answered those questions already subconsciously without you even knowing it. So, get to know your Values, and you will be able to determine the best direction at every step of the way to achieving your goals.

Anti-Procrastination Hack:

Knowing your personal values will give you the inner peace to always know which decision to take. Above all, they will make you happier and more successful.

Your Personal Values are fairly stable

Values, as said, are the things you value most. Values define what you find important, what you stand for. They guide our behaviors, decisions, and actions or in-actions. They are bound to a specific context, for example, a life-area, such as career, health or family. It might also be a Long-Term Goal. As you have defined your Long-Term Goals, I suggest that you start to determine your Values in the context of these goals. Values support you in achieving your goals. They are the driving force behind every step of the process finally resulting in you achieving your goal.

If you have achieved your Long-Term Goals and you choose some other Long-Term Purposes, it might be that related to these new Long-Term Goals a whole new set of unique values need to be developed. So, values are relatively stable over time because they serve your Long-Term Goals and they might change in the long-run because you chase new Long-Term Goals in the long-run.

Your goals determine the values you have. This is why it is a best practice to define your values in the context of your Long-Term Goals because then you can assure that your values are 100% supporting your goal. It is like a carriage with eight horses. The most efficient way is when all horses are running in precisely the same direction. When they are fully aligned with each other and with the coachman, who determines the direction.

Anti-Procrastination Hack:

Define your values in the context of your Long-Term Goals to make sure your values are fully aligned with those goals.

Step 1: Prepare yourself

The first step in defining your Personal Values is to Prepare yourself to explore your subconscious mind and to dig deep into the lower waters where the real power of your iceberg lie. So, make sure that you have decided to which Long-Term Goal you want to define your personal values. After that open up your mind. If you 're going to get to know your subconscious mind, then you need to establish a well-working communication between your subconscious mind and your conscious mind. The way to do this is to make space in your conscious mind. Your conscious mind can only contain seven plus or minus two chunks of information. So, if you want to let information in from your subconscious mind, your conscious mind better doesn't have too much on its plate. So, relax your conscious mind. Take a few deep breaths. Close your eyes for a few minutes and just watch how you are breathing. Just observe. That's all. This will calm your mind down.

Another critical thing to watch out for is being judgmental about what you will begin to explore. It is like Brainstorming 101: just let the flow of information come to you. Fight your urge to analyze your brainstorm ideas for as long as possible. Only when you are at step 4, your critical conscious mind may take it from there.

Anti-Procrastination Hack:

To prepare yourself to explore your Personal Values, clear your mind first, focus your mind on one Long-Term Goal, and withhold your critical conscious mind from stepping in too soon.

Step 2: Create Your List of Personal Values

Defining your Personal Values is an iterative process. You start very broadly and phase by phase you cut through them until you have your final list ready. So, first explore your values in the context of your Long-Term Goal and define as many values as possible. To help you get to know your personal values, it might be helpful to download my Personal Values List with almost 500 Values to choose from. You can download this list for free together with all the other book bonuses. Please, use the QR-code on page iv of this book to download them.

Alternatively, you could browse to:

https://SmartLeadershipHut.com/tapm-bonus

and download them!

I suggest using this list with personal values to help you get started. While this is a huge list of almost 500 values, you probably want to do this in five sessions or so, just to make sure you save your attention also for the last ones. In the accompanying free download, you also get an Excel file with the list of values. Personally, I have found it of great help to cut through this list and to mark each value which appeals to me with an "X" in column B. Moreover, while you will probably need more sessions to work on this list, the Excel file will help you to keep track of the values you have already dealt with and the values you still need to evaluate.

While going through the list of values, ask yourself this question:

In the context of my Long-Term Goal X, what do I find important?

I can imagine that after having read 50 values or so, your attention will drift away. As soon as you start to notice this, take a short break. Take a deep breath and again repeat the above question. It is essential to evaluate the values with this question in mind otherwise you will choose the wrong values.

The result of this step 2 is to bring the list of 500 personal values down to 50 to 100 values. Remember, we are iteratively doing this. This means that you perform your values definition in multiple rounds. This gives you the chance to re-think your values a couple of times. And every round you will achieve more clarity on your values.

Anti-Procrastination Hack:

Cut through the list of 500 personal values to create the first draft of your values in the context of your goal. Remember to focus your mind on this question while sieving through the list: "In the context of my Long-Term Goal X, what do I find important?"

Step 3: Bring down your list of values even further

Take the list you have created in step 2, and repeat the process of step 2 with this list.

By now you should have a list of no more than 50 to 100 values. So, the first round of sieving through all the values has already brought you closer to the clarity you want to have. Now, it's time for the second round.

Again, go through the list of now 50 to 100 values and ask yourself the same question:

In the context of my Long-Term Goal X, what do I find important?

For each value, you evaluate on the list, ask yourself: Is this important for my Long-Term Goal X? The way I do this is by copying first the tab in the Excel file to another tab. The first tab, I call "Round 1", the second tab, I call "Round 2". Now, sort the second tab for all the X's in column B. After that, delete every value without an X. Now, you have a list of only 50 to 100 values you can cut through for the second time.

Preferably, while performing this step, your conscious mind is still only observing what your subconscious mind will come up with. However, while going through the list of values again, you will find that some values have a very close meaning to you. In that case, choose the best one of the two which suits your goal in the best possible manner. For example, for my book project, I had in the first round chosen Accessibility, Approachability, and Availability. In the second round, I came to the conclusion that these three values were more or less the same to me in the context of my book project. From the three, I chose Accessibility because I find that if this value is fulfilled it, the other two will be fulfilled as well.

Another example is that I chose Confidence and Faith in the first round. In the second-round, I chose only Confidence because for me if I have Confidence in me finishing my book project, I will also have Faith. Furthermore, Confidence is more appealing to me than Faith. As said, this step is not meant to do an analysis, so don't worry yet, if you leave your list with multiple values which have more or less the same meaning to you. We will sort that out in the next step.

The end result of this step should be a list of no more than 20 values.

It might be that your list still contains much more than 20 values. In that case, I suggest to repeat Step 3 and cut again through the list. It might even be that you need to repeat Step 3 multiple times. Don't worry. This is pretty normal. I have this often too. Just repeat step 3 until you have cut down your list of values to around 20.

Anti-Procrastination Hack:

Cut again through the list of values, you narrowed down in step 2. Create the second draft of your values in the context of your goal. Remember to focus your mind on this question while sieving through the list: "In the context of my Long-Term Goal X, what do I find important?"

Step 4: Structure your values into a Values Hierarchy

For my Book Project, I had four values which are kind of similar or part of the same family: Nonconformity, Originality, Uniqueness, Vision. So, I want to group them into one more significant chunk. For example, Nonconformity, as a value, I asked myself "What is the goal in the context of my Book Project of having Nonconformity?". My answer was: Uniqueness. I want my book to stand out from the crowd, so, I want it to be unique. So, Uniqueness for me in this context is of a higher order than Nonconformity. So, I can easily skip Nonconformity because I know that it will be covered by the value of Uniqueness. I asked myself the same question for the value of Originality: "What is the goal in the context of my Book Project of having Originality?" Again, the answer was Uniqueness, so again I could easily skip Originality as a value. Lastly, I repeated the same question for Vision. The goal of having a great and compelling Vision in the context of my Book Project is for me Uniqueness. So, to summarize, the values Nonconformity, Originality, and Vision all are supporting values to the value of Uniqueness (in the context of my Book Project, of course). So, Uniqueness is for me in this regard the higher order value. However, the goal of Uniqueness is for me in this context Attractiveness. I believe that if my book is unique that it will also be more attractive to my readers. So, now I have a Values Hierarchy like this:

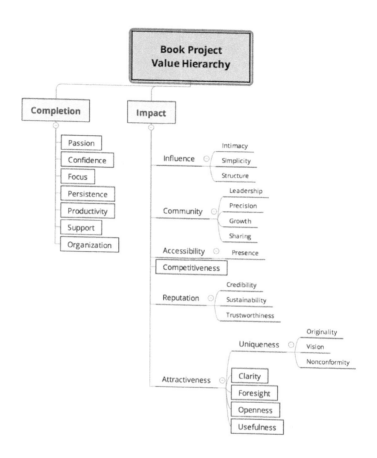

As you can see, I have 13 Values grouped into two Higher Order Values (Completion, Impact). So, the real core values of my book project are Completion and Impact. Everything else falls into one of those two categories. One of the ways to create impact for me is by having attractiveness. And attractiveness means for me being unique, showing clarity, and foresight, being open and useful. And by uniqueness, I mean having an original vision and being non-conforming. Do you see, how everything ties together?

The way to chunk your values is by asking yourself for each value on your list:

"What is the goal in the context of my Long-Term Goal X of this value?"

This will help you to see the higher order value which lies above the value you are evaluating. Now, you will start to see groupings of values, like in the example I gave. The end-result of Step 4 should be a Values Hierarchy like in the example above.

After you have drawn your Values Hierarchy, you can check the Hierarchy in two ways:

Top-down: Start with the top value and ask yourself what you need to have to fulfill this value. So, for example, one of my top values in the hierarchy is Impact. So, what do I need to fulfill this value? Well, the answer is Influence, a Community, Accessibility, competitiveness, Reputation, Attractiveness. Work your way down to the bottom of your Values Hierarchy. So, I need Attractiveness as a value to fulfill the value of having Impact. But what do I need to fulfill Attractiveness? Well, I need Uniqueness, Clarity, Foresight, Openness, Usefulness. And what do I need to fulfill the value of Uniqueness? That will be Originality, Vision, and Nonconformity.

Bottom-up: Start with the bottom of your Values Hierarchy and work yourself up to the top by asking yourself the question for each value: "What is the goal of this value in the given context?" So, for example, if I start with Clarity, then the goal of that is Attractiveness. The goal of Attractiveness is Impact.

So, to evaluate if your Values Hierarchy is correctly defined, it must be logically in both ways: top-down and bottom-up. If necessary, you can adjust your Values Hierarchy so that it will be correct. My suggestion is to perform this step in iterations too. This is because you need to let your subconscious mind have a chance to think it over as well. When you are asleep tonight, your subconscious mind will reconsider everything you did and thought today. Give your subconscious mind this opportunity; you won't regret it, I promise! After that, tomorrow, you can re-evaluate your Values Hierarchy, and the chances are that you will have new insights and conclusions. If so, just adjust your Values Hierarchy accordingly.

Anti-Procrastination Hack:

Structure your Personal Values into a Values Hierarchy by chunking your values up and down.

Step 5: Check your Values for Completeness

By now, you have your Values Hierarchy created and checked for consistency. But is it also complete? Or did you miss an important value? To check this, there are two important questions to ask yourself:

The Leave-question: Ask yourself:

"Within the given context of pursuing my Long-Term Goal X, and when having all these values in my Values, Hierarchy fulfilled, is there anything that could happen that will make me give up my goal entirely?"

Ask yourself this question and let your subconscious mind answer it for you. What comes to your mind?

When I asked myself this question with regards to my Values Hierarch I showed you in the previous step, it struck me that I was missing Money. Even when I have completed my book and published it and even when I have an impact on my audience, will I pursue my career as an author if I'm not earning any money with it? Well, my answer is No. So, the important value I have completely overlooked is Money. That's why I have added this value to my Values Hierarchy.

The Stay-question: Ask yourself:

"Within the given context of pursuing my Long-Term Goal X, and when having all these values in my Values, Hierarchy fulfilled, including the last ones added, what would have to happen such that would make me keep pursuing my goal?"

Asking yourself this question may result in an important value you haven't thought about before.

When I asked myself this question based on my earlier created Values Hierarchy and added the value of Money, my answer was that if I got requests from my readers for more books or other information, this would be a great motivation for me to keep writing new books. So, the value I have added to my personal values in the context of my Book Project is to get Reader-encouragement.

Asking yourself these two questions (Stay & Leave) will more likely than not give you one or more values which are very important to you and which you had not discovered otherwise. The reason that you have not thought about it earlier is that those values are most of the time hidden somewhere in your subconscious mind. That's the power of asking yourself this kind of questions. They reveal your own secrets!

Anti-Procrastination Hack:

Check your Values Hierarchy for completeness by asking yourself the Leave- and Stay-question.

Step 6: Analyze your Values Hierarchy

By now, you have mapped out your Values Hierarchy in the context of your Long-Term Goal. This means that you have made a map of a part of your subconscious mind. This map shows you how you think and what motivates you every step of the way. Usually, this map is invisible for your conscious mind. This means that you don't have a chance to analyze whether or not your Values Hierarchy is effectively working for you or not. But now you can! So, take the opportunity to examine your Mindset, because that's what we are talking about here. If you want to procrastinate less and be more successful, now you have the chance to improve all of that. So, let's analyze your Values Hierarchy and develop it for the better:

The question you should ask yourself when looking at your Values Hierarchy is whether or not this is supporting you for the full 100% in achieving your goal.

Let me give you an example. In the context of my goal to successfully publish this book, I have created this Values Hierarchy:

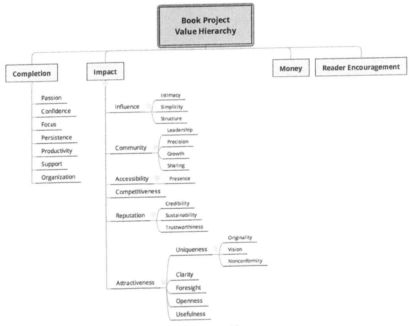

So, the question I asked myself was:

"In the context of my goal to successfully publish this book, is this Values Hierarchy supporting me for the full 100%?"

Well, first of all, I came to the conclusion that the Higher Order Values Money and Reader Encouragement needed to be further developed. Now, it is a too big chunk to get a grip on the meaning of it. The reason that these two values are not further developed if you recall is that these values came into my conscious awareness in step 5 where I asked myself the Stay- and Leave-question. So, the next step for me should be to repeat steps 1 to 4, but now specifically for these two values. So, instead of having the whole book project as a context, I can narrow down the context to specifically these two higher order values.

So, while going through the values list in step 2, the question I now should ask myself is:

In the context of my goal to successfully publish this book, what do I find important within the context of Money?

And after that, I should ask myself:

In the context of my goal to successfully publish this book, what do I find important within the context of Reader Encouragement?

If you are not 100% sure that your Values Hierarchy is helping you for the full 100%, then you know you have some work to do. This could, for example, be caused by some conflicting values in your hierarchy. Or it could be that some values are missing.

Analyze your Values Hierarchy for inconsistencies and omissions. Which important values are missing which you need to be successful in achieving your goal? Of all the values you have listed, are the dependencies and relationships in the best possible way? Now, it's time to use your critical mind and to take an objective look at your Values Hierarchy. If you notice that you procrastinate on doing the necessary tasks to achieve your goal, you can now analyze why this happens. Which values are you missing that causes this? Which values get more priority than others? Studying your current Values Hierarchy will give you awareness and insights why you are procrastinating right now. Maybe it is because you like to keep your options open and you don't want to say No to things or people?

Brainstorm for yourself how the most optimal Values Hierarchy would look like to be successful in achieving your goal. I know for sure that you are capable of doing this because it's not rocket science. Just give yourself the opportunity to think things over. A good practice is to repeat this analysis a couple of days later again. Your subconscious mind will have had the chance to think it over as well, so now you probably have some new insights. The end goal of this exercise is to design the best possible Values Hierarchy to achieve your goal.

Anti-Procrastination Hack:

Analyze whether or not your Values Hierarchy is supporting you for the full 100% in achieving your goal. For anything less than 100%, design your most optimal Values Hierarchy.

Step 7: Implement your Optimized Values Hierarchy

Designing an optimal Values Hierarchy is one thing, but more important is to implement it. You have mapped out from your subconscious mind your Values Hierarchy in the context of your goal. You turned it upside down and designed the most optimal Values Hierarchy possible to achieve your goal. Now, it's time to put your optimized Values Hierarchy back again where it belongs, your subconscious mind. This means that you need to build new neurological pathways in your brain aligned with your optimized Values Hierarchy.

For example, in the context of my book project, within the context of Money, I find it important always to see new opportunities to get my message across to my audience (aka YOU!). While this is something which is not "in my system" yet, meaning that I currently don't have neurological connections attached to that, this is something for me to implement. So, how do you do that?

The first step in implementing your optimized Values Hierarchy is to identify the gap between your old and new one. What are the fundamental differences? Write down the differences using positive affirmations. So, for example, you want to lose 10 pounds and be healthier. Your current Values Hierarchy has Fun, Joy, Pleasure, and Eating well as top 4 values. Now, you decide that these values are not helping your goal. So, you design an optimized Values Hierarchy with Exercise, Healthy Food, Action, and Excitement as top 4 values. Then you can define the gap between your old and new Values Hierarchy with the following positive affirmations:

- I like to exercise more than anything else.

- I always eat healthy food.
- I am taking action as often as I can.
- I'm totally excited when working out.

What would you think will happen to you when you fully believe that these four statements are true? You will value exercise, healthy food, action and excitement more than anything else. Instead of hanging on the couch and watching sitcoms, you will seek ways to move your body more, take more action, work out more. Instead of eating snacks, you will instead eat healthy food.

In the context of my book project, I wrote down:

- I always see new opportunities to get my message across to my audience.
- I always see new opportunities to reach new audiences.

The second step in implementing your optimized Values Hierarchy is to implement the statements you have written down into a new belief by ingraining it into your nervous system.

There are a couple of tools you can use for this:

- Make a Vision Board of your new values and beliefs so that they will become more tangible and concrete to you. Furthermore, repetition is vital to creating new neural pathways in your brain. So, the more often you visualize your new values, beliefs, and behaviors, the better this gets ingrained in your neurology. Therefore, it is a good practice to place your Vision Board where you can see it every day consciously and subconsciously.

- Visualize the new behavior you apply accordingly to your new values.

- Use Positive Affirmations throughout the day when you have moments that your conscious mind is idle. That's the power of positive affirmations. You can use them all day long, something which is a bit more difficult with visualizations. For example, when waiting at the doctor, or in traffic or even when doing the dishes, you can say positive affirmations to yourself. I repeat my positive affirmations probably a hundred times throughout the day, for example when I'm walking with my dog. And every time, my new beliefs and values get more incorporated into my subconscious mind and nervous system.

Repeat your visualizations and positive affirmations for at least one month. Repetition, as said, is key. Your old values are built probably over decades. Your mental energy follows the path of least resistance. So, the new neural pathways must be thoroughly ingrained and solid to bypass the old ones. Therefore, it is a common practice to repeat your new values and beliefs for at least one month. After that, your values and beliefs will be your new True North.

Anti-Procrastination Hack:

Use the two-step process to implement your optimized Values Hierarchy to support you in achieving your goal by using tools like a Vision Board, Visualization and Positive Affirmations.

Step 8: Use your Values Hierarchy on a day-to-day basis

As you will learn later in this book while developing your Process-thinking skills, the Eisenhower matrix is a very useful tool to evaluate all the activities, ideas, requests, emails, and so on, you get on your plate on a day to day basis, so that you know where to say Yes to, and, more important, where to say No to. One of the important distinctions you need to make with this decision matrix is whether or not an activity is important to you. However, even when you know what activities are important to you, you can't do them all on the same day, most of the time. So, how do you decide, which of the activities are extremely important, and which are "regular important"? This is where you can use your Values Hierarchy of your goal. Your Values Hierarchy will determine which activity has more importance over others. For example, if I have only one-hour free time in my agenda today and I have to choose between writing a new article for my blog or writing a new chapter in my book, I will choose for the latter. As you can see in my Values Hierarchy above, Completion is my most important top value. So, writing a new chapter which brings the completion of my book nearer, is far more important to me than writing a new article on my blog. The latter is also important to me because it is adding up to my value of Presence and Leadership and finally Impact. But the value of Impact is a little less important to me right now than the value of Completion.

To implement this thought in your day-to-day life, I suggest that you print out your Values Hierarchy and look at it regularly. Your Values Hierarchy should become "a living document" where your regularly refer to and also make regular additions and clarifications to. The more you will use your Values Hierarchy the more it will come to life and the more power and motivation it will deliver you.

Anti-Procrastination Hack:

Let your Values Hierarchy guide you through your day when deciding which activities are important enough to complete.

Develop Process-thinking skills to get stuff Done

This chapter focuses entirely on Process-thinking. This is one of the two components of The Anti-Procrastination Mindset. Always remember, that you need to balance Results-thinking with Process-thinking. You can read more on that in the previous chapter. But for this chapter, the scope is only Process-thinking.

What is Process-thinking?

With Results-thinking you focus on the end-result. You focus on what is ready when you have achieved your goal. With Process-thinking, however, you focus on all the activities which have to be done to get that end-result. Process-thinking focuses on the journey you have to make to get to your final destination. What do you have to do to get there? What will you encounter along the way? Do you have to deal with obstacles? Can you avoid them? How do you avoid them?

Based on your quarterly goals, you define the activities necessary to accomplish your quarterly goals. Furthermore, you identify the interdependencies between the activities, so that you know which activities are a prerequisite for other activities. This all ends up in an activity planning for the coming weeks.

Once per day you perform Process-thinking to decide what you have to do that day and to evaluate how your past day went and what you need to optimize. The goal of Process-thinking is to plan the activities you need to perform in such a way that the chance of you being successful, in achieving those tasks, will be maximal.

So, Process-thinking consists of three main steps:

- **Step 1:** Evaluate your past day
- **Step 2:** Plan your current day
- **Step 3:** Create an outlook for the next seven days

Step 1: Evaluate your past day

If you can optimize your day with only one percent, and you repeat that day after day, then after one year you will be a whole new person. You will be 37 times more successful, effective, and efficient. Only one percent each day, that's all you need!

In the chart below, you can see that when you start at the beginning of the year at level 100, that you will end up at 3,700 just by optimizing yourself with one percent each day:

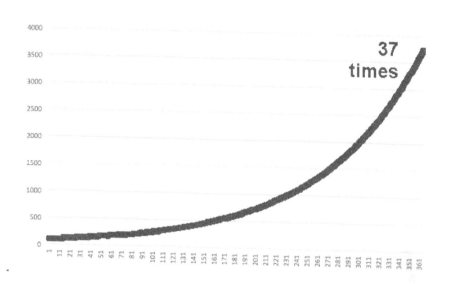

To optimize yourself with one percent each day, you need to evaluate your past day and ask yourself what went well and what can be optimized. Don't look for the big things. Look for the small wins. The goal is to optimize yourself with one percent. So, evaluate your day and brainstorm what small gain you can implement right away. This might be a checklist you make, a template, a new small routine, whatever. Try it out and see what works and what not. And after a couple of days, when you have your daily evaluation, ask yourself if you want to keep your new habit when it is effective. One small win every day will improve your life tremendously!

Step 2: Plan your current day

Have a look at your activity planning, so that you know what activities you have to perform today. Now, visualize your day. Make an internal movie of how you will walk through your day. See yourself in the picture.

See yourself doing the very first activity, and then the next and so on. See, how well you are performing the various activities. Also, notice possible roadblocks and ask yourself how you can prevent them. Ask yourself how you will deal with obstacles effectively when they show up. See, how you will successfully go through your day and accomplish all the activities, you have planned.

I plan my activities in chunks of 20 minutes. This keeps me entirely focused on the action, and it is also motivating to check off a lot of activities. Every time, I have finished one of those activities, my brain releases dopamine which motivates me to start with the next activity. Furthermore, the hurdle to performing a 20-minute activity is much lower than for any other activity. Almost every 20-minute activity is part of a more significant task, of course. But I simply plan the very first step which can be done within the scope of about 20 minutes or so. After I have finished the activity, I immediately plan the next step I can accomplish within 20 minutes. The way I do this, is by using Evernote. For example, when I want to publish a new article on my website, this consists of a series of activities. In an Evernote note, I sum up those activities, like a checklist. Then I decide on the very first step I can perform within 20 minutes. As soon as I have accomplished that step, I decide on the next 20-minute step. I make a note of that in Evernote, and after that, it might be that I'm doing some other work. But as soon as I have planned to continue with my article, I refer to the Evernote note, and immediately know crisp and clear what to do next. This works highly motivating for me, and I suggest that you try this out as well.

Another advantage of having 20-minute tasks defined is that when you have some spare time, you don't have to become idle. Just pick one of the tasks, and accomplish them within 20 minutes.

Anti-Procrastination Hack:

Plan your activities in sprints of 20 minutes. This makes it easy to fill small spaces of time left with doing something useful. It also makes starting an activity easier because it is manageable.

Step 3: Create an outlook for the next seven days

When you plan your day, also have an eye on the activities you need to perform the next seven days. It might be that due to the progress you have made, a shift in your planning will be necessary. In that case, reshuffle your planning accordingly. This might also mean that it is required to perform an activity already today which you had scheduled for another day.

Anti-Procrastination Hack:

Schedule a fixed time every day to perform Process-thinking. Evaluate your past day, plan your coming day and have an outlook on the next seven days. Plan your tasks in chunks of 20-minutes to keep you motivated and to get stuff done.

Process-thinking gets your stuff Done

With Results-thinking you are focusing on the end-result. However, without doing the hard work, you will never achieve that end-result. That's why you need Process-thinking as well because that will help you focus on what exactly you have to do and how you have to do it, to achieve your goal. As said above, with Process-thinking you will visualize your day in such a way that it will be easier to go through your day while accomplishing the tasks you need to do that day. It will be easier because you will have seen yourself finishing the tasks successfully and you will have identified possible obstacles and found a way to deal with them effectively. So, before you have actually started your day, you will have diminished various types of resistance you would have generally encountered throughout your day. And with less resistance, it is much easier for you to start actually doing what you have to do. So, instead of procrastinating on things because you want to avoid the frustration you expect, you will be motivated to start to work on your goals because you will find it promising, enjoying and fulfilling.

With Process-thinking, you will also use Positive Affirmations as a tool. So, when you plan your day in the morning, and you are thinking of the difficult email you have to write today or the frustrating meeting you have this afternoon with your colleague who always wants to pick a fight with you or the invoices you really need to pay today which you don't like, then you will automatically feel resistance against all those activities. Not very tempting, isn't it? So, the chances are that you will procrastinate on those activities and instead seek some less important things to do. However, if you will visualize that these activities are already finished successfully, then the resistance against those activities will diminish.

For example, you visualize that the meeting with your colleague will be the best meeting you have ever had. How will that look like? And how will you feel after the meeting is finished? Imagine yourself feeling great after this successful meeting. Furthermore, you say to yourself "The meeting with Jack this afternoon has been very successful for both Jack and me!" Repeat this affirmation a couple of times for yourself while feeling great. Can you imagine, that your resistance against that meeting will be gone? So, instead of hesitating to go to that meeting and seeking reasons to cancel it, you will be looking forward to that meeting.

Anti-Procrastination Hack:

Process-thinking gets stuff Done. It will take out your resistance against the activities you have to perform, and it will help you see the successful outcome of your activities. Less resistance and more motivation equal less procrastination and more stuff done.

The 15 Process-Thinking Strategies

In the next paragraphs of this chapter I will discuss the following Process-Thinking Strategies in detail:

- Define your short-term tasks and goals
- Deal with the urgency paradox effectively - Continuously Optimize Yourself
- Don't get yourself overwhelmed
- Prioritize your activities with great care (Your Time is Valuable!)
- Procrastination is like an Invisible Enemy
- Make starting the first tiny little task your goal
- Everything gets easier when you break it down
- Work in small intense sprints on your task
- Tap into your reserve tank and get used to feeling uncomfortable (the real key to willpower)
- Become aware of your Urge to Procrastinate
- Get a head start with temptation bundling
- Which Stonecutter are you really?
- Find an Accountabilabuddy
- Say NO to competing goals, projects, tasks, and obligations

Anti-Procrastination Hack:

Study every one of the 15 Process-Thinking Strategies to help you get stuff Done.

Define your short-term tasks and goals

Once per week, you have a Weekly Review meeting with yourself where you plan your next week based on your quarterly goals. If you know what needs to be finished within 13 weeks, you also know what needs to be finished next week. Put everything which needs to be finished on a task list for the coming week. Use this list once per day to decide what needs to be done today. Write down the tasks which need to be done today on your daily to-do list. Make sure that you especially clearly define what the very first step is which needs to be taken to start the activity. So, what is the first tiny next step?

Defining the very first tiny next step is very important because this will help you to start easily with your planned activities instead of procrastinating on them. And once you have completed that first little step, the following steps will follow quite automatically. See, also this Process-Thinking Strategy.

For example, if you need to have that meeting with your colleague, then the first step will probably be to get yourself to the meeting room where you have your appointment. Clearly visualize how that will look like. What do you need to bring with you? Your notepad and pen? Your laptop? Both? Anything else you need to take with you? How will you go there? Visualize exactly how it will look like if you are going to the meeting room. This will make it super easy for you to start the activity because not only do you exactly know what to do and how to do it but you have also seen yourself doing it successfully. So, where is your procrastination now? There is no procrastination! There is only you doing what needs to be done!

You also use your Weekly Review Meeting with yourself to evaluate your past week. What went well and what could be improved? Did you accomplish your weekly goals? If not, what needs to be done next week?

Anti-Procrastination Hack:

Use Process-thinking to plan your weekly and daily tasks based on your quarterly goals. Make sure you visualize the very first step of each task for today so that starting that task will be very easy.

Deal with the urgency paradox effectively

As I have already mentioned earlier in this book, despite having an anti-procrastination Mindset and having planned your goals and activities perfectly, life can easily get in the way. This is a fact which you should always take into account when planning your day because otherwise you get disappointed and frustrated and that will ruin your day anyway.

There are all kinds of unexpected things that can require your immediate attention. And they often have the potential of transforming into something more catastrophically, especially when you don't deal with it efficiently and immediately. So, this means that it is really necessary to deal with those situations immediately and wipe your agenda clean.

As soon as something unexpected happens during the time that you have planned to work on your activities, ask yourself these questions to evaluate how urgent it is:

- What is the worst-case scenario if I don't immediately deal with this situation?

- How will this situation impact all my other goals?

- How will this situation impact my family and friends?

- What are the less important activities I can put off?

- What are the actions I can take today to resolve this issue?

The aim here is to put things into perspective. As said earlier, No Goal is an Island.

The paradox in handling unexpected issues during the day is to judge whether something needs your immediate attention or not. You can't ignore urgent matters, of course, and at the same time, you can't use unexpected issues or things as an excuse to procrastinate on your important tasks. That's why it will help you to ask the above questions to put things into perspective.

Anti-Procrastination Hack:

Put urgent matters into perspective and find the right balance in handling them immediately vs. not letting yourself be distracted.

Continuously Optimize Yourself

Controlling your reptile brain and overcoming your procrastination is not accomplished with overnight success. It is like building a new habit. It requires your conscious attention every day over the period of a few weeks. Therefore, I suggest that you do daily visualizations of your future-self (see the chapter about Future-Self Visualization).

Furthermore, I advise you to review on a daily basis how you are making progress towards becoming a goal getter and stopping your procrastination temptation. You can do this by planning a daily review meeting with yourself. This only takes 5 or 10 minutes where you go over your day. Ask yourself the following review questions during this daily review meeting:

- What did I plan to accomplish for today?
- What did I do well to accomplish this?
- What could I have done better?
- Were there any urgent interruptions today?
- How did I dealt with them?

- What could I have done better?

I do this every day when I walk home from my office. So, it doesn't have to cost you extra time on your calendar.

There are two possible outcomes of this review meeting. Either you are very happy with what you have accomplished and how you have accomplished it. Or you are disappointed with how you did it. In the last case, it is important not to beat yourself up. Just say to yourself: "Needs work." This way you will start to use your creative brain to develop methods and solutions to improve your next day.

Anti-Procrastination Hack:

Optimize yourself continuously by reviewing your productivity progress on a daily basis. Use the review questions to evaluate your day. If you are happy with your results, great! If not, optimize yourself by saying: "Needs work!"

Don't get yourself overwhelmed

When my wife starts a new project, like cleaning the house, redecorating the living room, or making a photo album of our last holiday, she always thinks that she can do everything in one go. All the activities related to a particular project, she wants to finish in a couple of hours or a day at the max. And then when she starts next day, she is totally confused about what she should do first, overwhelmed by the sea of activities laying in front of her resulting in doing a lot and achieving nothing. And furthermore, she gets heavily disappointed when she comes to a conclusion halfway the day, that she has done a small portion of what she intended to do. This is the big danger of planning too many activities in your day. Instead, it would benefit her if she would plan only the most 3 important tasks. This is easier to focus on and easier to get started. All other less relevant activities can then be done when there is time left.

Anti-Procrastination Hack:

When you plan your day, identify the top 3 most important tasks you want to accomplish. This should be your primary focus. Aim to do those tasks first thing in the morning, so that you will be energized to work on other things the rest of the day.

Prioritize your activities with great care (Your Time is Valuable!)

An average human being has continuously too much on his plate to complete. If you only look at the enormous amount of emails and social media messages you get every day! It's nearly impossible to handle everything with the greatest care. More importantly, do you want to handle everything? As you hopefully know, your inbox is everyone else's agenda but yours. This is why you need to prioritize your activities so that you have at least enough time left in your schedule to work on the goals which are important to you. But how do you evaluate quickly what to work on and what not? This is where the Eisenhower matrix comes in handy.

> *"Being busy is a form of laziness, lazy thinking and indiscriminate action."*
>
> Tim Ferriss

The Eisenhower matrix is named after Dwight Eisenhower, the 34th President of the United States, serving two terms from 1953 to 1961. Eisenhower lived a highly productive life. Before he became president, he was a five-star general in the United States Army and served all kinds of other high profile jobs. He was capable of maintaining high productivity for decades. The Eisenhower matrix is one of his famous productivity strategies. Using this matrix, you can very simply, quickly and effectively take a decision on what activity to do and what not to do.

It works very simply. You can divide every activity in important versus not important. Furthermore, you can divide each activity into urgent versus not urgent. This leads to a matrix with 4 quadrants:

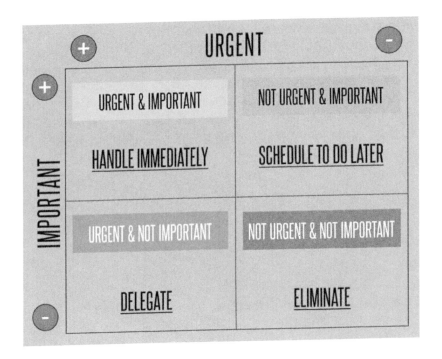

Q1: Urgent and important

Tasks which you should immediately do because they are critical in the context of your life and goals. Often, you need to do these tasks to avoid more severe negative consequences. These tasks need to be done before you can work on any of the other quadrants of the Eisenhower matrix.

Q2: Important, but not urgent

Tasks which you can schedule to do later. These tasks are often related to your Long-Term Goals. Ideally, you want to invest most of your time working on these tasks because they have the most benefit for you. But while these tasks are often not time-sensitive you can easily put them off to do later if you need to work on Q1 priorities.

Q3: Urgent, but not important

Tasks which you can delegate to someone else. These are often the tasks that someone else asked you to do but are not related to any of your goals. For this kind of tasks, the question is not when or how the question is "Who?"

Q4: Neither urgent nor important

Tasks which you should eliminate immediately. The tasks in this quadrant only serve as a distraction and withhold you from achieving your goals.

You can also use the matrix for evaluating which goals you want to work on and which not. In that case, you should read "goals" where it now says "tasks."

The difference between Urgent and Important

According to Eisenhower, what is important is seldom urgent and vice versa. So, what's the difference?

Important tasks: the tasks that contribute to your Long-Term Mission, Goals, and Values.

Urgent tasks: the tasks that you think you should react to immediately. For example, if someone is calling you for the second time in 5 minutes.

How to distinguish Important versus Non-Important Tasks

Distinguishing urgent versus non-urgent tasks is quite simple. However, distinguishing important versus non-important tasks is often quite difficult.

To know whether a task is important to you, you need to be very clear about what your short-term, mid-term and Long-Term Goals are, what your values are in the various contexts of your goals, and what type of person you want to be.

Furthermore, there is often also a priority amongst your goals. Many goals might be important to you, but some goals are more important than others. This is why I advise you to prioritize your goals and values into a goals hierarchy and values hierarchy.

To get started with the Eisenhower matrix, I recommend you to print out an empty matrix, like this one:

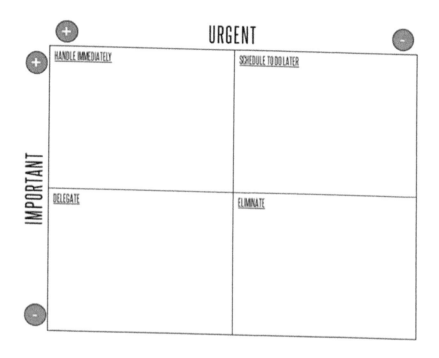

You can download an empty copy of the Eisenhower matrix for free together with all the other book bonuses. Please, use the QR-code on page iv of this book to download them.

Alternatively, you could browse to:

https://SmartLeadershipHut.com/tapm-bonus

and download them!

Use one blank diagram per day. When planning your day, use this diagram and put your goals and activities in each of the four quadrants. This will already give you a good feeling about your priorities. So, when all kinds of unexpected things happen during your day, just evaluate shortly where the particular event fits into your diagram. And, of course, act accordingly upon it.

Ultimately, you should only spend your time in quadrants Q1 and Q2. Evaluate once per week, based on all your diagrams, how you have performed. Rethink about the way you handle your priorities and take the decision to improve yourself the week after.

Using the Eisenhower matrix will help you to get perspective on what's really important for you and to choose wisely on what you spend your time on. The result of this is that you will be more decisive based on your core values and goals. You will be a better goal-getter, and you will procrastinate much less.

Anti-Procrastination Hack:

Spend your time only on activities which are important for you and your goals. Use the Eisenhower matrix to decide what you should work on and what not easily.

Say NO to competing goals, projects, tasks, and obligations

There will always be all kinds of distractions on your way to achieving your goal. Often, they are disguised as opportunities or joyful things to do. The variety of disturbances is immense. This is a fact of life. But how do you deal with these distractions effectively? By now, you have your Long-Term Goals clearly defined. Your True North is waiting for you in your future. You also have your Quarterly Goals identified so that you will be very clear about what you have to do the next coming months.

So, now you exactly know what to focus on. Everything else, you have to say No to. But how do you deal with that when you are continuously bombarded with distractions?

What if you have suddenly the chance to start a very compelling and joyful new hobby? Or what if you suddenly have a brilliant idea what you can do with your home decorations? There are so many things which cross your path and which are very fun to spend your time on. But unfortunately, this will have a negative influence on your Long-Term Goals. Everyone has only 24 hours in a day. Even the wealthiest and the most successful men on earth. The big question is, how to spend your 24 hours in a day wisely. My suggestion would be, to spend your valuable time only on goals which are the most important to you in your life aka your Long-Term Goals.

> *"I am as proud of what we don't do as I am of what we do. People think focus means saying Yes to the thing you have to focus on but that's not what it means at all. Focus means saying No to the other hundred good ideas there are. You have to pick carefully, so saying No to the thousand things is your key to success."*
>
> *Steve Jobs*

If you are like me, you probably find it also difficult to Say No to joyful things. They sound so very promising and seem to be so much joy, why say No to something so good? My father, he is 80 years old now, wants to make a documentary about his hometown Dordrecht in The Netherlands. He has been a local tour guide in the city for ages and also been a video amateur for ages. And now he wants to combine those two significant hobbies of him into this new project. However, he gets stuck in the project. So, I was thinking of helping him out with this project. Usually, being enthusiastic about the idea of helping my father, I would have jumped immediately into it and also in the process of doing that having committed myself to finishing the project. However, I decided to evaluate my decision first and take a step back from it. I wrote down the pros and cons of this idea, let the idea rest for a few days, and after that re-evaluated the pros and cons. While living about 200 miles from my father, it would take me way too much time, I don't have right now, so I decided to not follow up on this idea, which sounded promising in the first place. [Update: luckily my father got in the meantime unstuck, and he even managed to win the first prize with his movie at his local video club]

"Most of the time, the initial spark of things will vanish after a second look."

So, what I did was taking a step back from the blissful idea and looking more objectively at it. By waiting a couple of days and allowing my critical mind to step in and sum up the pros and cons of the idea, I was able to detach myself emotionally from the concept and make a more objective evaluation possible. The advantage of that is that you take your whole picture in mind when deciding to take on a new task or goal or not. Now, you will be able to keep your Long-Term Goals top priority and say No to all other projects, ideas, goals, task, or adventures which are not adding up to your Long-Term Goals. The prerequisite, of course, is that you have a clear vision of your Long-Term Goals which we already have covered in a previous paragraph. The outcome of your evaluation doesn't have to be always No, of course. It might also be that the new initiative or idea you have, is really adding up to one of your Long-Term Goals. In that case, you should take this action on board in your Long-Term Planning, maybe as one of your quarterly goals.

Anti-Procrastination Hack:

Don't procrastinate on the goals which are most important to you. Instead, learn to say No to competing projects by evaluating new ideas and initiatives before committing to them.

Procrastination is like an Invisible Enemy

Procrastination is a nasty temptation. Lots of tasks are not fun to do but nevertheless require little effort and can be done quickly. For example, doing the dishes, or responding to that email. And yet, often you put this kind of tasks off. This may seem like no big deal because what is the harm in doing the dishes later? Or responding to that email later? They are short activities anyway. But, actually, this is a big deal. Putting things off is a temptation which can turn into a nasty habit and stay that way. Even if you are putting off the smallest task, it all adds up in your head to the list of your procrastination habit. It has nothing to do with what you put off. It has all to do with the fact that you didn't resist the temptation to procrastinate.

Procrastination is like an invisible addiction. That's why it is so hard to fight it. It is like smoking cigarettes one after another without even consciously being aware of it. The difference is that you later become aware of the full ashtray or the empty pack of cigarettes. And then you know that you have smoked a lot of cigarettes. However, if you later see that you still have to do the dishes, you probably don't think "Oh, that's due to my procrastination habit." No, instead, you are probably irritated and think something like "OMG, I still have to do the dishes! Okay, let's watch Netflix first." This means that although you may procrastinate a lot during the day, you are not aware that you are doing it. And this is not helping you because this means that it is difficult to fight your procrastination. Procrastination is like an invisible enemy! And that's very hard to fight against with!

The disadvantages of putting off small things which could have been done quickly, are worse than you think:

- Your habit of letting your procrastination temptation ruin your day is fed every time you put off even the smallest thing.

- The task you have put off is burning mental energy until you have completed it.

- The task you have put off becomes bigger and bigger in your head the longer you wait to complete it.

So, don't fall into the procrastination temptation trap and complete little tasks as quickly as possible. A rule of thumb is the two-minute rule of David Allen. He recommends that tasks which can be done within two minutes should be done immediately without thinking about it. So, every time some to do item pops into your mind, ask yourself if it can be done within a few minutes. If yes, then do it immediately. Unless of course, you are already heavily involved in another activity which you better complete first. Then make a note, and do the task immediately after you have finished what you are working on right now.

Anti-Procrastination Hack:

Do quick tasks which can be completed within a few minutes immediately or as soon as your current task is finished. Don't let procrastination become your invisible enemy!

Make starting the first tiny little task your goal

One of the reasons that you procrastinate, as we have discussed earlier, is that you tend to avoid cracking the hard nut. As soon as it gets a bit difficult, as soon as you need some extra mental or physical energy for a task, you tend to put off the task. I don't blame you for that, of course, because I do this also, like all the time. It's a natural reaction. The point is that you need to become aware of it. No one wants to do unpleasant things. This is simply because your reptilian brain is preventing you from doing harmful things as a means to the survival of your body and genes. Of course, you would rather do something pleasant instead. This gives you instant gratification which releases dopamine into your body and makes you happy.

Most of the time, you avoid cracking the hard nut because you have made the task too big in your head. For example, on my website SmartLeadershipHut.com, I have a blog. My goal is to blog every week. But often, I find it very hard to write a new blog post. Why? Because I don't like to write? No, that's not the case. It's because I made the process of blogging way too complicated. I had made a list of things to do for each blog article.

Here it is:

- Write article of at least 2,000 words
- Edit article
- Check article for Grammar issues
- Choose URL
- Design in Thrive Architect
- Full-Width post
- Featured Image: 1080x330px
- Heading 2: Font-size: 30px / Line-height: 40px / Top-margin: 60 / Bottom-margin: 25
- H2 Images: 1080x330px / Full-width / Top-margin: 60 / Bottom-margin: 70

- Heading 3: Font-size: 26px / Line-height: 33.8px / Top-margin: 60 / Bottom-margin: 25
- Take the Quiz below picture
- Click to Tweet / Font-size: 16px / Line-height: 40px / Top-margin: 60 / Bottom-margin: 70
- Quick Navigation
- Internal links
- External links
- Quiz: 3 questions
- Conclusion
- Lead Magnet
- Over to you section
- Rich Snippets
- Videopal
- Youtube Video Embed
- Animated GIFs
- Tags
- Category
- Schedule

Do you see how overwhelming this is! So, every time, I thought about blogging, this whole list popped into my mind's eye, but then ten times bigger! And, already I was tired and frustrated even before I had started. Not a good strategy!!

Even more frustrating is that on the one hand I lost all my appetite for blogging but on the other hand I still wanted to keep blogging consistently.

So, I changed my strategy. I decided to skip the list. I designed a minimum viable blog template and made it a habit of spending at least 10 minutes every day on my blog. Just 10 minutes. And this works pretty well because now I spend time on blogging every day and it excites me again. And the results are also good because since I used this new strategy, I already posted a couple of new articles on my blog.

When the going gets tough, the tough get going. But what to do if you aren't tough already? Simple! Don't make things so tough! If a task is complicated, time-consuming or simply tough, start by defining the very first tiniest little easy peasy task. And then focus on completing that task. Because as soon as you have completed that tiny little task, all the other domino stones will start to roll over as well. Even the biggest and toughest one, if only you place them in the right order. And for that to make that happen, you need Process-thinking.

81

Anti-Procrastination Hack:

Starting and completing complex, time-consuming, and annoying tasks is easy. Instead of focusing on the big and ugly domino stones, find that one little tiny domino stone which is easy to start and complete and which has the power to throw over all the other domino stones. Make starting the first and tiniest task your primary goal. Design your day around that.

Everything gets easier when you break it down

I am an IT Project Manager for over 25 years now. And one of the important tasks of planning each project is breaking the project down into small bite-sized tasks. This is Project Management 101, of course, but there is an important lesson in that: **Everything gets easier when you break it down**. If a task is too big, it is overwhelming, it is hard to plan, and it is hard to complete.

So, as soon as you are confronted with too big a task, don't get yourself overwhelmed. Instead, ask yourself how you can break the task down into small chunks. Make sure that the chunks of tasks can be completed within one hour or so. This makes them easy to schedule in your planning and easy to start and complete. I break-down tasks even further in chunks of 20 minutes because that is the amount of time I can be fully focused on just one thing before losing my concentration.

I am not a favorite of making large to do lists. Often, they get a life of themselves without serving you. However, when it comes to breaking a project down into small bite-sized chunks, there is no other way then to make a list. Even the smallest project can add up easily to ten tasks of one hour. Don't expect yourself to hold all those ten tasks in your mind and prioritize them as well. Just write them down. Make a fishbone diagram, for example. This is a diagram starts with the end result in mind.

For example, let's assume that you have to give a presentation next week for your senior management. Instead of feeling overwhelmed by the idea only, break it down. Start by asking yourself what the end result should be. For example, the end result is to convince your senior management to give the approval to implement the new process you have developed.

Now, ask yourself what you have to do to accomplish that goal. For example:

- Create a storyline for your presentation.

- Develop the PowerPoint slides.

- Ask preliminary feedback on your presentation from important stakeholders.

- Send the presentation at least two days before the presentation to your senior management.

- And so on, you get the picture.

Now, ask yourself if the activities on this level can be accomplished within one hour or so. If not, break them down even further until you have activities that can be accomplished within one hour or so.

Now, schedule all the activities on your agenda. As soon as the first activity needs to be done according to your agenda, you will exactly know what to do, how to do it and that it is easily feasible to accomplish by you within one hour. This is much more motivating to start working on than something like "Make a presentation." So, the chances of you starting and completing what you have planned to do will be much higher!

82

Anti-Procrastination Hack:

Use a tool like a fishbone diagram to break down your project into small bite-sized chunks which can be

> *accomplished within one hour. Everything gets easier when you break it down.*

Work in small intense sprints on your task

If you have followed along with the previous anti-procrastination hacks, then, by now, you should have a list of bite-sized tasks which can be accomplished within one hour or so. It should not be very difficult for you to start this task. The question is now, how do you stay focused on the tasks, so that you can actually complete it?

Already in the early 1990s, Francesco Cirillo described a technique called the **Pomodoro technique**. He called it Pomodoro because he used a tomato-shaped timer to track his bursts of focused, concentrated work. As soon as you start working on your task, set a timer for 25 minutes. Most smartphones have this option nowadays, so this shouldn't be too difficult, I suppose. The aim is to fully focus on the task for 25 minutes and then take a short 5-minute break.

When I started using this technique, I must admit that I was not able to focus for 25 minutes long on one activity without getting distracted by all kinds of things. That's why I decided to train my focus. I made special background music which helps you focus and concentrate. I made tracks of 5, 10, 15, 20, 25 and 30 minutes. I first started with the 5-minute track. And I aimed to focus fully on the whole five minutes without getting distracted. After I succeeded in doing that, I leveled up to 10 minutes and so on. Today, I find myself happy to focus for 30 minutes without getting distracted. If you'd like, you can download these tracks of Stay Focused Music for free toegether with all the other book bonuses, so that you too can benefit from it.

Please, use the QR-code on page iv of this book to download them.

Alternatively, you could browse to:

https://SmartLeadershipHut.com/tapm-bonus

and download them!

The Pomodoro technique aims to focus for 3 cycles of 25 minutes, with a short 5-minute break in between and then have a longer break. This helps you to stay focused, motivated, energized, and creative.

The Pomodoro technique works because it is hard to focus for a long time. And now you only have to be focused for small intense bursts of 25 minutes. Furthermore, it helps you beat your procrastination temptation because it is only a small amount of time. So, it is easier to start and easier to complete. This is especially true if you design your day into work-packages of 20 minutes like I do because then you exactly know what to do in one burst of focused work. Last, but not least, this technique helps you to become more consciously aware of how you plan and spend your time.

Anti-Procrastination Hack:

Work, in short, intense sprints of 25 minutes on your task (Pomodoro technique). This helps you to beat your procrastination temptation and increases your focus.

Tap into your reserve tank and get used to feeling uncomfortable (the real key to willpower)

The more you get used to feeling uncomfortable, the more successful you will be. If you learn to master feeling uncomfortable, the sky is the limit, and you can master almost anything. You can certainly overcome your procrastination temptation and become a goal getter.

No one likes feeling uncomfortable, me neither. But the thing is that if you want to develop yourself from a procrastinator into a successful goal-getter, you need to seek discomfort. Routines are good. They can make you highly productive, certainly good routines. They make you feel in control and at ease. However, they dull your sensitivity. I'm sure you have that experience too. You drive every day the same route to your office. It gets boring very quickly. After a while, you tune out and start thinking about other things. Or you listen to music or a podcast. But what you don't notice anymore is your environment on your way to your office. This is the danger of living and being in your comfort zone. You tune out and stop sensing what's going on around you. For a short period of time, this is no big deal. But the world around you keeps spinning around. Fast! So, before you know it, you are detached from your environment. You make decisions with the old assumptions which aren't a reality anymore. Few people like to feel uncomfortable. However, discomfort is the way to go when you want to develop yourself. Developing yourself means doing things differently than you used to be. "Used to be" means comfort. "Differently" means discomfort. So, what if you could learn to embrace the feeling of discomfort? If you could enjoy being uncomfortable? Then you would be more resistant to doing new things, don't you think? The challenge is to get yourself over the hurdle of wanting to return to your comfort zone. Once you have passed that hurdle, you are free to experience new things, do things differently, think differently and grow. Your body will create brand new neural pathways which will spark your creativity, enhance your memory and also make you happier. This is because putting yourself in new and unfamiliar situations triggers the release of dopamine. This is the chemical which makes you happy.

Discomfort brings engagement and change, according to Seth Godin. "Discomfort means you're doing something that others were unlikely to do because they're hiding out in the comfortable zone."

Anti-Procrastination Hack:

See discomfort as a way to develop yourself and achieve your goals. Discomfort is your friend. Don't' shy away from it! Embrace it! It is the only way forward.

Here is how you can leave your comfort zone and feel comfortable with being uncomfortable. When you feel uncomfortable, focus on something else. Feeling uncomfortable is an emotion. And emotions are controlled by your thoughts. The big question is when you feel uncomfortable, what are you thinking that makes you feel like that? And after that, to stop thinking that thought because then you won't feel uncomfortable anymore. This is easier said than done. Unfortunately, it doesn't work like that. If I say to you "Don't think of a Blue Tree!" Then what is the first thought you have? Exactly! The Blue Tree! Instead of saying what I don't want, it is better to say what I do want. So, if you are still thinking of that blue tree right now, and I don't want you too, it would be better to ask you to think of a purple tree, for example. Or of a red cow. Or blue ocean.

For three years in a row now, I take a cold shower every morning. There are all kinds of speculations that this should be good for your health but that's not why I do it. I do this every morning because I hate it! I never get accustomed to it, even after three years. But this is my morning ritual to leave my comfort zone on purpose and to train myself in controlling my fight or flight response. The first couple of months, every time I took a cold shower, I got all kinds of negative emotions and panic attacks while taking a cold shower. I must admit that I still have a remaining of it although it is only a fraction of what it was. Luckily, I discovered two things to control my fight or flight response. The first one is that instead of taking a cold shower unprepared, I had to prepare myself mentally in such a way that I was expecting the negative emotions and panic attacks. So, I became very realistic about the emotions I could expect when leaving my comfort zone. The funny thing is that when you expect them to come, they are much less intense because you have kind of detached yourself slightly from your emotions. The second thing I learned is to keep my conscious mind busy and to focus on something completely different. To that, I started counting. "One-Mississippi,

Two-Mississippi, Three-Mississippi," and so on. My target was to count to 50. By doing this, I focused my mind on something else which prevented negative thoughts from popping into my mind. Well, sort of, because my thoughts are much quicker than I can count. So, every now and then a negative thought pops up. But in comparison with the situation before, it is now just a fraction of what it used to be.

So, if you focus on something completely different, other than the thing you are feeling uncomfortable about, your mind gets occupied with other thoughts. And very soon, the thought which made you uncomfortable is out of your head. And the accompanying feeling will also be gone.

Another thing you can do to feel comfortable being uncomfortable is to make a brain dump of everything which is bothering you. Writing it down takes it literally out of your head and onto the paper. You have dissociated yourself from what is bothering you. Now, you can look more objectively at it. Analyze it. Break it down into small bite-sized action steps. And decide when you start working on the first one.

85

Anti-Procrastination Hack:

Dissociate yourself from your discomfort feeling. Focus your mind on something else. Focus your mind on the goals you want to achieve and the results you will reap from that. Write your feelings down and analyze them. Define your first bite-sized action step.

Often you feel uncomfortable because you need to do something which didn't go so well in the past. And now you are afraid that this will be a predictor of your future and that you will fail again. I can imagine that this functions like a big red flag for you, which will motivate you to procrastinate and deny it. According to Martin Seligman, our failures don't determine our future success. No, it is how we **explain** our failures to ourselves. So, write down your past failure and find an explanation why it didn't work out so well back then. And at the same time, find an explanation for yourself that your failure will be limited to that occasion only. While you have learned from it, all future occasions will be successful. This will motivate you to do what you should do and feel comfortable with it at the same time.

This is again, the big difference between someone with a Procrastination Mindset and someone with an Anti-Procrastination Mindset. The first person will think that his situation is as good as it gets. He identifies himself with his failures. The second person with an Anti-Procrastination Mindset knows that his future is malleable and that he always can improve himself. He doesn't identify himself with his failures. Instead, he learns from them and embraces them.

All successful people have failed miserably multiple times. But the reason they are successful now is that they have found a way to learn from their failures and counter their discomfort. And this is something you can do too.

Anti-Procrastination Hack:

Learn from your past failures, but don't let these define your future. Instead, see them as a lesson for future success.

There is, by the way, a fine line between feeling uncomfortable and feeling panic. If you are panicking you have gone too far out of your comfort zone, and that's not what I'm asking you to do, of course. But playing it safe, and always staying within your comfort zone is neither an option. Or, according to Mark Zuckerberg, the world is changing so fast, that there is no other way than constantly taking risks. Because if you don't take risks, you will fail anyway, because old habits, skills, ways of working, and so on are not applicable anymore.

To avoid the panic mode, start with small challenges. Pick an activity you'd rather not do and feel uncomfortable with, but at the same time which isn't that hard. See it as an exercise in developing yourself.

For example, I don't like vegetables. I hardly eat them. At the same time, I know that eating vegetables is healthier for me than anything else. Furthermore, I used eating vegetables as an exercise in feeling comfortable with being uncomfortable. Because eating vegetables is totally not my cup of tea. So, every morning when I wake up, the first thing I do is to eat 3 leafs of spinach. I don't like it, but nevertheless, I do it.

It helps me to dissociate myself from my feelings. I say "Harry is eating spinach. Harry doesn't like spinach. Harry feels disgusting."

Anti-Procrastination Hack:

Train your discomfort muscle with small challenges and avoid the panic mode.

Learn how to access your reserve tank. Do you think that you know yourself well enough to know how far you can go? Well, according to American Navy Seals, you don't. Whether you are exercising, studying the piano, writing that report, as soon as you feel that you have done enough, that you have no more concentration or energy left, you are lying to yourself. If you are telling yourself that you are done, you are actually only at 40 percent done. You are much more capable of doing things than you think you are. You only have to push through the urge to quit. Control your fight or flight response!

Therefore, three is a magic number. If you have the urge to give up, don't! If you have the urge to give up the second time, don't! If you have the urge to give up the third time, then go. This how you train to control your urge to give up too quickly, because, remember, you always have 60 percent left in your reserve tank! You certainly don't want to be the stonecutter in the picture you saw earlier!

Anti-Procrastination Hack:

Learn to access your reserve tank by not giving up the first and second time. You have always 60 percent left, the first time you think you are done.

Become aware of your Urge to Procrastinate

If you are not aware that you are procrastinating, then it is difficult to change it. So, the very first step, in every change for that matter, is becoming aware that you procrastinate. You might think right now, "But, hey, I am aware of it, why else would I have bought this book in the first place?" Ahum ... yes, you have a point. I understand. But are you aware of your procrastination habit in all instances? It is like the habit of eating sugar. Most of the time, you are not aware that you eat something with sugar in it. Your procrastination habit is often very subconsciously hidden so that you hardly notice something as actually procrastinating.

Please, have a look at the 30 Signs that you are a Procrastinator, from the first chapter of this book. The chances are that there are a lot of examples of things that you perceive as "normal" but in fact are a sign of procrastination. For example, the sign "You tend to take on more than you actually can handle." You probably think "Well, yeah, but that's because I am a doer. I like to keep myself busy. That has nothing to do with procrastination." Well, is it?

If you are really honest with yourself and answer the question, why you tend to take on more than you can handle, what will be your answer? The chances are that the real reason is that you want to have an excuse for yourself for not doing some other important activities. And the big question now is, if you know what those activities are? And after that, you can analyze why you are procrastinating on these activities and use the appropriate anti-procrastination hacks of this book to counter that.

So, be aware of your procrastination. Analyze your behavior and then stop your procrastination habit. To help you with that, I suggest that you download the Checklist with the 30 signs that you are a Procrastinator. Print this checklist and use it to evaluate your daily activities. For every one of the 30 signs, ask yourself if that happened lately. And if so, what was the cause? What was the real culprit that this happened? If you do this daily, or at least regularly, you will be much more aware of how and how much you procrastinate. Furthermore, you can track your progress in your development from procrastinator to goal getter. After a couple of weeks, you will start to see that your urge to procrastinate will be less and less every day. Don't expect this to happen in the first week. When you start with training your awareness of your procrastination habit, you will probably see an increase in procrastination. That's not because you are getting worse. It is simply because your awareness grows. So, you start to notice things, you were not aware of before. And that's a good thing!

Anti-Procrastination Hack:

If you don't know that you procrastinate, it will be hard to fight it. Use the 30 signs that you are a Procrastinator to become more aware of your procrastination temptation.

Get a head start with temptation bundling

During the start-up phase, a motor accelerates more and draws more power than when it is normally operating. This is a law of physics. In fact, it is Newton's first law of motion: "An object at rest stays at rest; an object in motion stays in motion; with the same speed and in the same direction unless acted upon by an unbalanced force."

Getting started with an activity is always the hardest part. Even for things you perceive as motivating and pleasurable. That's why Katy Milkman, assistant professor at Wharton University, researched and developed a technique called temptation bundling.

Temptation bundling is where you piggyback on a temptation you already have. So, for example, a temptation of yours might be to watch your favorite

Netflix series. What if you could combine this temptation with something you must do but rather procrastinate on? Your mental motor will be already in operation before you even know it.

I use this myself when walking to my office. I can go to my office in two ways: walking or biking. Walking gives me a longer period of being in motion, so I think that's healthier for me. At the same time, I'd like to listen to podcasts which is something I don't like to do on my bike. So, I decided to start walking to my office, so that I could listen to a podcast every day. So, in essence, I killed two birds with one stone. I move more and get to listen to podcasts more. And the one doesn't happen without the other. As soon as I start to listen to a podcast, I walk.

So, temptation bundling is to couple something you really like to do, for example watching a particular TV series on Netflix, with something you want yourself to do but have trouble starting with, for example working out. You use the temptation of watching your TV series as the starting engine to work out. You can't do the one without the other. You have to make a deal with yourself that you will not watch that particular TV series without working out at the same time. So, now every time you have the urge to watch your TV series, great! Go for it! But not without working out at the same time! So, your TV series have become now a motivation and a trigger to do something you would normally procrastinate on doing. As soon as you stop working out, you should stop watching your TV series. Do you like to know what will happen next in the series? Great! Now you have a reason to look out for your next work out session!

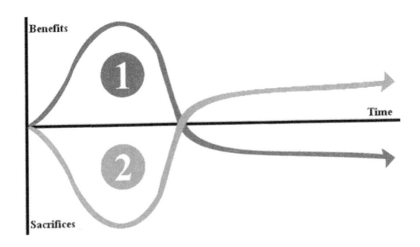

As you can see in this diagram, there are two types of activities:

Activity Type 1: doing these activities give you an immediate benefit, an instant gratification. Like watching Netflix, for example. However, after the short boost in feeling happy, the effect of this type of activities declines and will turn into a long-term loss. This type of activities are often the bad behaviors we have. We all know what they are. They provide us a quick benefit or enjoyment in the beginning, but with long-term negative consequences.

Activity Type 2: doing these activities will ask sacrifice of you in the beginning. But in the long-run, they will provide you with benefits. The big mistake most people make is that they quit this type of activities too early so that they will never reap the benefits and only feel the sacrifices. This is why it is so important for you to persist and follow through on these activities until you have them completed and achieved your goal. Often, type 2 activities are the good behaviors we want to develop, as our new year resolutions. They are the activities that are always important but never feel urgent.

Temptation bundling makes it easier for you to accomplish type 2 activities. Use your guilty pleasures to pull you in, so that it will be easier for you to follow through on the more difficult type 2 activities.

You can couple every temptation with every activity you know you have the habit of procrastination for. It is just a matter of designing your life more productively.

So, start making a list of all your temptations. Also make a list of the activities you know you want to do or should do, but procrastinate on. Now, find creative ways to couple a temptation activity with a must-do activity.

Here are a couple of "house-rules":

- Write down your decision to couple the temptation activity and the must-do activity.

- Decide that you only will allow yourself to perform the temptation activity when you will do the must-do activity at the same time.

- Decide that you will stop your temptation activity immediately when you decide to stop your must-do activity.

- Evaluate once per week on how you follow through on your own decisions.

- If necessary, course correct.

A couple of years ago, I followed a course on privacy regulations. I had to learn a lot of legal stuff. Boring! So, what I did was, I put the things I had to learn by heart in Evernote so that I had access to it on my phone. And every time I went for a walk with my dog, which is at least two times per day, I learned some stuff. So, I coupled something I enjoy, walking my dog, with something I had to do. Not only that, walking my dog is an activity which I regularly perform anyway. So, this gave me the chance to learn my stuff on a regular basis in small bite-sized pieces.

Do you remember the Eisenhower matrix? Well, the second quadrant with tasks that are important but not urgent is ideal to use with temptation bundling. This type of activities is not urgent so you can postpone them easily until you want to watch your favorite TV series, for example. But at the same time, these activities are important enough to work on them regularly. So, while you have coupled them now to some tempting activities, you can be assured that you will not put them off endlessly.

Anti-Procrastination Hack:

Use one of your temptations, like watching a particular TV series, as a starting engine for a must-do activity. Combine both activities. Only if you start the must-do activity, you are allowed to do your temptation activity as well. And as soon as you stop your must-do activity, you have to stop the other activity as well.

Which Stonecutter are you really?

Some 800 years ago a lonely traveler happened upon a group of stonecutters. They were cutting stones adjacent to the river the traveler had just crossed. Curious about what the stonecutters were doing the traveler stopped and asked one of the stonecutters what he was doing. "I'm cutting stones, can't you see that?" was the grumpy answer he got. "Okay, apparently, this man is not in a good mood," the traveler thought, wondering if all the stonecutters were like that. When he arrived at the second stonecutter, he asked the same question again. This stonecutter paused for a minute, straightened his back and said: "Well, I'm cutting stones so, that I can support my family." "That's great!" answered the traveler and after a short conversation he left off. By the time the traveler approached the third stonecutter, he already heard him shouting at him. "Did you see it? You must have seen it?" The enthusiasm of this worker was contagious, so by now, the traveler had become very curious. "What should I have seen dear fellow?" he replied. "The Cathedral we are building" responded the man enthusiastically. "You must have seen it on your way here." "No, I'm afraid I took another route. So, you are building a Cathedral?" "Yes," the stonecutter replied. "We are all cutting stones to build that Cathedral! Isn't that beautiful!" "Please, point me the way, so that I can see it for myself," asked the traveler. "Sure!" and after the stonecutter had given the traveler the right direction, he went quickly on with his work.

In this little metaphor, there are 3 stonecutters who all do exactly the same work. The big difference between the first and the third stonecutter is that the last one sees the bigger picture. He is not blinded by the stones he has to cut every day. Instead, he is highly motivated by adding the building the Cathedral. Which stonecutter do you think is happier? Which one does enjoy what he is doing? That's right! The one who sees the bigger picture and who knows how he is adding value to that. Let this be a lesson for you too. Start seeing the bigger picture.

If you can relate the tasks you need to do to an important overarching goal of yours, you will suddenly feel more motivated to start to work on it. Therefore, it is a good practice that when you procrastinate on something, to ask yourself "How does this task relate to any of my important goals?"

There are two things important when you want to answer this question:

- You need to know your important goals.
- - You need to know that you are procrastinating.

If you come to think of it, practically everything you need to do relates to some important goal or value of yours. You only have to be conscious of it. That's all. So, anything you are avoiding right now can turn into something motivating and exciting because it will add up to something bigger. Start building cathedrals instead of just cutting stones!

Find an Accountabilabuddy

I don't know about you, but funny enough, I perform better when I have to do a project or task for a customer instead of just performing a task for myself. In both situations, the activities or projects may be very important, but when you have to do it for a customer, it becomes more urgent than when you just want to do it for yourself. But is it just the urgency, or is there more? I think that it also counts that you feel a certain obligation when you must do a task for someone else than just yourself. What do you think?

This is why it helps to have an accountabilabuddy. I remember the time when I was in University (in the good old 1980s!). As a college student, you have no customers. You only study for yourself. So, as an initiative of the University, there were all kinds of study groups. I was a member of one of those groups myself. Every week on Tuesday afternoon we came together. And all we did was present to each other what we had planned to do for last week, how we performed on our planning, and what we planned to do for the next week. A kind of, what they call nowadays, an agile way of working. By presenting this to our fellow students, we created a kind of accountability. When I went next week to this group again, I didn't want to say that I had done nothing! So, I did my best to follow through on my own week planning. And my fellow students did too.

All anti-procrastination hacks in this book are based on internal motivation, except this one. In this case, the motivation for you to do what you have planned to do and not to procrastinate is external. It is driven by accountabilabuddies who help you to keep you accountable for your planning.

Accountability is your attitude of continually asking yourself what else you can do to exceed the expectations others have of you. It is the process of seeing it, owning it, solving it, and doing it. This requires having ownership, commitment, and thinking in solutions instead of problems.

If you feel accountable for achieving a particular goal, then it will almost be impossible to procrastinate. You will be unstoppable driven to your goal. As said, all anti-procrastination hacks in this book are designed to develop that accountability for yourself, so that you will be unstoppable too. However, it is also possible on some occasions to create external accountability. All you have to do is find someone who wants to keep you accountable for keeping your promises and achieving your goal.

There are many ways to have an accountability partner. You can ask a close friend for example. But you can also blog about your goals and the way you are achieving them and let your followers be your accountability partner.

There are also accountability services on the internet. After signing up, you can state your goal and when you want to have achieved it. You also pay a certain amount of money. This will be released to you when you have achieved your goal. However, if you don't succeed in achieving your goal in time, they will pay the money to a charity you hate. So, this is a very much pain avoidance driven motivation.

We all like to have a witness in our lives. Your parents were your first witnesses of your life. They have followed and cheered you up on all your developments until you were old enough to leave them. After that they still followed you, of course, but now from a distance. So, you were looking for other witnesses to follow your life. Like your close friends and spouse. Without a witness, our lives would be meaningless. This is why post so often on social media about our current status. And this is also why having an accountabilabuddy is a strong motivator.

So, think of a goal you really want to accomplish but have difficulties with persisting on it and not procrastinating on it. Brainstorm for yourself if someone you know could help you for this particular goal, to be your accountabilabuddy.

Would you like to join our special VIP Facebook group with like-minded people, such as you, who held each other accountable? It's free!

Simply, follow the QR-code at the end of this book or, alternatively, browse to :

https://www.facebook.com/groups/slhcommunity/.

91

Anti-Procrastination Hack:

Seek an Accountabilabuddy to support you to follow through on your goals and to be more accountable.

Develop Process-thinking skills to get stuff Done

Balance Results-thinking with Process-thinking

The **Anti-Procrastination Mindset** is a Mindset where you find the right balance between Results-thinking and Process-thinking.

It is a bit dependent on where you are in your project and on the type of project, but often you should be focusing like 5% of your mental energy on Results-thinking and 95% of your mental energy on process-thinking.

These are not hard figures, of course. It is just a way of expressing that both ways of thinking are important and should be used simultaneously, but process-thinking should get by far your most attention.

If you are procrastinating right now, it might be caused by the total absence of Results-thinking, Process-thinking or the wrong balance between both ways of thinking.

Procrastination due to no or wrong Results-thinking

If you don't apply Results-thinking, then you don't plan. If you don't plan, then there is nothing to postpone. So, you would think that the failure of Results-thinking is the ideal recipe to no longer have procrastination. But unfortunately, that is not the case. The opposite is true. If you don't use Results-thinking, that's the ideal recipe to encourage procrastination for yourself.

If you don't apply Results-thinking or if you apply Results-thinking incorrectly, you will not know the requirements necessary to achieve your goals. So, for example, you have set yourself the goal of running the next New York marathon, but without thinking about what you need for it. So, how will you determine if your goal is feasible or not? For example, you don't know whether you will be in shape in time to run the marathon or that you will have enough time to train for it. You also don't know whether you can take leave by the time the New York marathon is scheduled to travel to New York. Just as you don't know whether you will have the financial means to pay the travel and accommodation costs. You probably also have no idea what it will be like to run a marathon. Maybe you don't like it at all.

The incorrect application of Results-thinking means that you might be very busy, but with the wrong things. Maybe you start running the next day, but because you don't have all these other things on your mind, the chance of failure is higher than the chance of success. And you may only find out when you have not reached your goal. Then you can say that you have failed. Although it is not procrastination, it is failure behavior. But often the feeling of failure occurs much earlier in the process because your subconscious mind knows that you miss a large part of the puzzle. And because you don't know what the puzzle should look like, you will either panic or ignore it. And this, by definition, results in procrastination. Why would you bother to train every day for a marathon you feel is far out of your league?

92

Anti-Procrastination Hack:

Use Results-thinking to help you see the big picture and estimate early if your goal is feasible and what it takes to achieve your goal. Otherwise, you will increase the chance of failure and procrastination.

Procrastination due to no or wrong Process-thinking

It might be that you procrastinate because you don't use Process-thinking or that you use it in the wrong way. Let's turn our example of you wanting to run the New York marathon around. You have used Results-thinking extensively, so you now exactly know what running this marathon requires from you. You also have a solid plan in place to make this come true. So, very enthusiastically, you go to bed with the plan to train first thing in the morning. But, as soon as your alarm clock goes off, you feel too tired to start your training. So, you put it off until tomorrow. What harm can be done when starting one day later, right? But let's be a bit more optimistic about ourselves. You have put on your running shoes, and you have already run for ten minutes or so. And suddenly you start to feel a cramp in your ankle or so. Or it starts to rain. Or you feel too tired to go on. Did you know, that when you say to yourself that you have given yourself for the full 100%

and that there is nothing left in you to pursue, that you actually only have used 40% of your reserve tank? This means that you still have 60% left when you want to give up training. The big question is, will you finish your training or give up on it?

Using Process-thinking will allow you to deal with all kinds of obstacles on your way to your goal effectively. So, everything from getting up early to train, to coming home and taking a shower after your training, you need to be able to handle. You do this by applying negative visualization which will be discussed in further detail here. This will help you detect all kinds of possible obstacles at forehand. "What if I'm too sleepy to get up early? What will I do then? What if I'm too tired to get up? What will I do then? What if I can't find my running shoes? What will I do then? What if it is raining? What will I do then?" and so on.

If you encounter many obstacles during the day which gets you frustrated and stressed out, then you know that you must pay more attention to your Process-thinking skills. Because otherwise, you might easily get disappointed or frustrated which causes you to either procrastinate or give-up entirely.

93

Anti-Procrastination Hack:

Don't let your frustrations and disappointments make you procrastinate or give-up entirely. Instead, see them as a signal that you need to use your Process-thinking more or better. Challenge yourself to develop your Process-thinking skills.

So, both ways of thinking are important to use and should be balanced effectively.

Process-thinking is the way of thinking where you focus on the hard work part of the equation. What are the activities which need to be done on your way to your goal? What do you have to do today to move the needle in the right direction?

Anti-Procrastination Hack:

Hard Work times Many equals Result. To know which hard work you need to do, you need both Results-thinking and Process-thinking. To actually perform the hard work, you need Process-thinking.

Be aware of the Stockdale Paradox

During the Vietnam War, Admiral James Stockdale was shot down. He spent almost eight years in a brutal prison camp.

Naive optimism got you killed in those camps, according to Stockdale.

Some guys thought they'd be out by Christmas. But when Christmas came and went, they still were kept in prison. So, they thought they would be out by Easter. Easter came and went, and they still were in prison. And then they lost hope and died.

The guys who survived were thinking in a totally different way. They knew that they would eventually be free and they knew it was not going to happen anytime soon.

Stockdale himself knew that he would be at least five years kept in prison, but he knew the day would come that he would be free again.

This is called The Stockdale Paradox.

- On the one hand, you need to have utter confidence that you will inevitably succeed.

- On the other hand, you need to accept whatever brutal reality you are facing. Your path to success will not be easy, and it will not be short. This is why it is so important to know, understand and acknowledge your current situation.

You need to find the right balance between focusing on your end goal and focusing on the process goals for today. Sure, you also need to focus on your big end goal. That's the one hand in the Stockdale Paradox. But this should only 5% of your focus at the max. The other 95% of your focus should go to the other hand of the Stockdale Paradox which is to focus on your daily process goals.

Luckily, I have never been in prison, like James Stockdale. But when I was eight years old, I had a similar situation. I suffered from a severe brain tumor. The hospitals in my city couldn't treat me for that, so I came in a hospital in another city than where I lived. After three months and a couple of surgeries, I was released. But for the eight-year-old version of me, this seemed like ages. And in this strange big hospital in another city, I was very homesick. The only thing I was thinking every hour I was awake, was: "I want to go home!" So, every doctor who came to my bed, and they were countless, I asked: "When may I go home?" Most of the time, they said something like: "Maybe next week." But when next week came, I still had to stay in the hospital. You can imagine that this drove me crazy and that I had lost all hope for the future. Now, 44 years later, I still have troubles thinking about my future. So, I thought the opposite of how Stockdale thought. I was so concerned with the end-result of getting out of the hospital that I couldn't stand the harsh reality of every day, every surgery, every medical examination, all those blood samples they wanted to have from me, and so on. In hindsight, my life in the hospital would have been so much easier and better if I had accepted my current reality from day one. But hey, I'm only human!

95

Anti-Procrastination Hack:

Be aware of the Stockdale Paradox and find the right balance between focusing on your end goal and focusing on the process goals for today.

How to balance Results-thinking with Process-thinking?

If both Results-thinking and Process-thinking are well-balanced, then chances are that you don't procrastinate often. You are also well-motivated most of the time. You are successful in achieving your goals. You set goals, and you achieve goals. You are a real goal getter!

If, however, you are too focused on Process-thinking, you probably do like a headless chicken all kinds of activities. You might think that you are very busy, but are you really moving the needle? It might also be that you are not working on your goals at all because you are not motivated.

Most of the time you only need process-thinking because you need to do all the hard work necessary to achieve your goals. But in times when you are bored or annoyed by the work you need to do, for example, administrative work, it is time to use results-thinking to motivate yourself to start working.

Anti-Procrastination Hack:

To stop procrastinating and become successful in pursuing your goals, you need both Results-thinking as well as Process-thinking. But you need to balance both in the right way.

How to switch to Process-thinking?

The first thing to become aware of is that every result you see in your life is the end effect of a series of actions you have taken. Have a look at the diagram below:

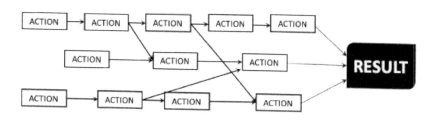

As you can see, each action leads to another action. And some actions can't be started before an earlier action is completed. In the end, when all actions are completed, you get a result. But what if you are not happy with the result? For example, because the result comes too late, has not enough quality, or has cost too much? Then this is a consequence of the actions you have taken before and the way you performed those actions.

You can also look at it the other way around. If you do once per day your daily evaluation of your day and you come to think of things which went wrong or not so well that day, then that are all examples of results. Results as a consequence of actions you have taken. So, for example, if you were late for work, then this is a result. Now, you can reverse engineer this result to find out why it was that you were too late. What were all the actions you have taken to achieve that result? So, for example, you got out of bed at 6:00 a.m. You followed your normal morning routine, left the house at 7:15. Walked to the bus. Took the bus at 7:23. Arrived at your work at 8:10. Walked to your office and got started at 8:17. Which is 17 minutes later than you planned to do. So, now you can ask yourself which of the different steps you can improve to be sure you can start your work next morning at 8:00 a.m. sharp. Do you have to take a bus earlier? What do you have to do to take a bus earlier? Walk faster? Leave your house earlier? Track down the step which needs to be improved and take the decision to improve on it. And starting tomorrow morning, you will not be late for work anymore.

97

Anti-Procrastination Hack:

Every result is a consequence of a series of actions. Process-thinking means that you are aware that you can only change your result by changing your actions. Track down the actions which need to be improved and start improving them.

If you want to switch from Results-thinking to Process-thinking, then you have to stop your Results-thinking. With the previous example in mind, it has no use to keep thinking about you being late at work It also has no use to hope that you will be on time tomorrow. Or to complain about the traffic jam. Or the weather. Or whatever. That are all examples of Results-thinking.

You don't change your results with Results-thinking.

So, you need to stop your Results-thinking and start with Process-thinking. To help you with that, you can lay a piece of paper and a pen aside from you. Every time, your mind starts throwing ideas at you which are Results-thinking type of thoughts, write them down and say to yourself: "Later!" And after that, continue with what you were working on. This way your mind gets heard. Possible valuable thoughts don't get lost. And by writing them down, you clean your head, which makes it easier for you to continue with Process-thinking.

Sometimes, it might happen that you can't clean your head. That's no problem because I have a very effective technique for that which is called the Visual Squash. Use that and you can re-focus on the task at hand and start doing the work you need to do.

Anti-Procrastination Hack:

You don't change your results with Results-thinking. Instead, you need to stop with Results-thinking and start with Process-thinking, if you want to get better results.

Another important thing you can do to use more Process-thinking is to evaluate once per day how you have done that day. Just view your day from start to finish and ask yourself which obstacles, annoyances, frustrations, disappointments, moments of stress you have encountered. And after that, ask yourself why you had not seen that coming. Is it because something totally random happened which you absolutely could not have foreseen? Or, is it simply because you were not using Process-thinking? Now, ask yourself how you can improve on preparing your next day.

Anti-Procrastination Hack:

Once per day, evaluate how you have balanced your Process-thinking with Results-thinking. Evaluate, based on what went well and what went wrong that day, and take new decisions for the next day.

Very important to start with Process-thinking is to know what the next steps are you need to take on your way to achieving your goal. Because each of those next steps determines the scope of your Process-thinking. How do you determine the next steps? Well, with your goal in mind you ask yourself what the first upcoming milestone is. Every big project, like running the New York marathon, for example, has several milestones. In this example, it might be that you are able to run the 5 miles and that you have figured out where you are going to stay in New York. So, now you have only two milestones to focus on. For each of these milestones, ask yourself, what need to be done first? And then you brainstorm about the next steps. The result of this is a list of next steps, you can put in the right order and plan them in your schedule. Remember, this list should only focus on the tasks you need to do the next couple of days.

Now, you are all set to proceed with the real Process-thinking on each of these tasks. If you'd like to know, how, then please read on:

Anti-Procrastination Hack:

To be able to do Process-thinking, create a list of next steps you need to take for the upcoming days, for each of your goals.

How to do Process-thinking or Results-thinking

With both ways of thinking the aim is to focus on a goal. However, when you use Process-thinking, your goal is something you want to accomplish within the next couple of days, while with Results-thinking it is something you want to accomplish within the next weeks, months or even years. By definition, your Process-thinking will be more specific, while your Results-thinking will be more generic.

Running the New York marathon is a big goal you want to accomplish within a couple of months with hundreds of underlying activities and so on. While running five miles today is a very concrete goal with only a couple of activities necessary.

For both ways of thinking you focus on a goal. You look at the goal, its implications, obstacles and so on.

Step 1: Define the Scope of your thinking process

If you are Results-thinking, choose what the scope of your thinking will be. It will probably be a mid- or Long-Term Goal you want to achieve. Let's call this goal "X."

However, if you decide to start Process-thinking, the scope of your thinking will be to accomplish a task in the next upcoming days. Now, let's call this task also "X."

The result of step 1 is that you have chosen a goal "X" which is either a short-term goal or a long-term goal depending on whether you want to use Process-thinking or Results-thinking.

Step 2: With regards to the chosen scope "X" ask yourself the following questions:

- What are the positive outcomes when I have accomplished X?

- What are the negative outcomes when I have accomplished X?

- What will be the impact of accomplishing X for myself, my family, friends, stakeholders, and eventually the world?

- What are the possible obstacles on my way to accomplishing X?

- Use Negative Visualization to brainstorm all possible things that can go wrong with X.

- What can I do to prevent the obstacles from happening?

- If, in any case, an obstacle will happen, what will be me the most adequate response to deal with the obstacle effectively?

Asking yourself this type of questions upfront will help you to be well-prepared to accomplish X, and it will set you up for successful achievement of X without having to procrastinate on it or to give up on it.

Anti-Procrastination Hack:

To start with Process-thinking or Results-thinking, use the two-step process. First, define the scope of your thinking, then ask yourself the different questions within the chosen scope.

Create your daily Strategic Thinking routine

People like Warren Buffet and Bill Gates spend a great amount of their time thinking about their life and business. Tim Armstrong (AOL's CEO) takes this even a step further. He makes his executives think about their business 10% of their day. Jeff Weiner (LinkedIn's CEO) schedules even 2 hours of uninterrupted thinking time every day. Why do these successful CEO's spend so much time on thinking? Well, simply because this is the best and only way to get a clear vision and gain direction and focus on your life and business.

Balance Results-thinking with Process-thinking

Strategically thinking time, every day, is your best chance to gain and remain a clear Vision, Direction, and Focus in your life and business.

If you want to stay focused, then you first need something to focus on. And it better be something important, because your concentration is extremely valuable! To know what to focus on, you need direction. And you get direction by thinking strategically ... a lot! Like in photography, focus has everything to do with vision. So, the first step in creating more focus is to create a clear vision.

Schedule a time every day for strategic thinking. Use this time to evaluate how you are doing.

At least ask yourself every day this question:

"What's the best thing I could be working on, and, why am I not?"

This is a very important question because it combines Results-thinking with Process-thinking in the right way.

I also schedule strategic thinking time every day. Every morning from 6 am to 7 am, I sit down with pen and paper. I write down my big goals for the coming 12 months. I spend time thinking about my important values. And I spend time thinking about my "I am's." This last one is about what type of person I want to be. For example, "I am an author." Furthermore, I spend some time being grateful for where I am right now. And I set my goals for the upcoming day. Performing this kind of results-thinking every day gives me an enormous amount of energy and motivation.

Your strategic thinking time is one of the ways to "sharpen your saw" as Stephen Covey has called this principle. As you know, you can't always go on and on and on. You have to recharge your batteries. And to recharge your mental energy and focus you need time to think and reflect.

Anti-Procrastination Hack:

Schedule a daily meeting with yourself where you think strategically about the way you use Process-thinking and Results-thinking effectively and how you can improve on that.

Face the Negative Outcomes before you even have started

"You must prepare yourself by previous thinking out and practicing how to act in any emergency or accident so that you will never be taken by surprise."

- Robert Baden-Powell

By thinking upfront about all the possible negative outcomes your goal could have, you will never be taken by surprise. This means that whatever will happen when you are working on your goal, you will be prepared for it. This gives you an enormous feeling of control because you know upfront that you can handle everything. What, do you think, will be the impact of this on your level of confidence? It will boost your confidence level! This is why already the Roman emperors practiced negative visualization, this is how this practice is called, a lot. And not only to be well prepared for any future event, but also to be happier right here and right now, about their life.

There are two ways in which you can benefit from practicing negative visualization:

1. Practicing negative visualization gives you more perspective on where you stand right now with regards to your goal. This makes you happier about yourself in general and about your goal specifically.

2. Practicing negative visualization prepares you for every imaginable situation and consequence while working on your goal. This is why you can be more confident because you already have proof for yourself that you will be able to manage it.

Both advantages of practicing negative visualization lead to more focus and determination on working on your goals and less procrastinating on them. Performing negative visualization will reduce your fear of failure, fear of success, and fear of the unknown. Instead, it will boost your confidence, productivity, success, and happiness.

Chesley Burnett "Sully" Sullenberger III is called a hero because he managed to land US Airways Flight 1549 in the Hudson River off Manhattan on January 15, 2009. Shortly after the plane had taken off, it was disabled by striking a flock of geese. All 155 people aboard survived. According to Sully, however, it was all due to adherence to procedure why he could rescue the plane and of course the teamwork with his co-pilot Jeff Skiles. Both pilots had never flown before together. So, how did both exactly manage to do what they had to do when the plane started to crash? Well, long before they flew off while sitting on the runway at LaGuardia Airport, they went through a series of checks. They first introduced themselves to each other and then they walked through all kinds of checks. And ... they also discussed what to do when a terrible disaster happens, like if the engines fail. Both pilots had 25 years of experience and never had any engine failed. And both probably expected that this would also never happen. Yet, they still went through their checks and because they did when the plane started to crash they had just three minutes to manage the situation and all chaos broke loose. But they then exactly knew what they needed to do and how they were dividing their tasks.

Both pilots used negative visualization as a standard procedure. This made them very resourceful when it was necessary the most. Without this type of visualization, they would probably not be equipped to land the plan on the Hudson River so well.

Negative visualization is the practice of using worst case scenario type of expectations and visualizations to see through the surface of only the positive side of things. Negative visualization allows you to put off your rose-colored glasses and see the world as it really is. It allows you to bulletproof yourself against things with a negative impact that might happen.

If you would only think positively, then you will be disappointed again and again by unexpected things which will happen. This will, of course, urge you to say yes to your procrastination temptation. So, instead, expect shit to happen, because it will. Nearly every situation ends differently than we have expected due to all kinds of unforeseeable things which will happen.

"Misfortune weighs most heavily on those who expect nothing but good fortune."

- Seneca (Roman Senator and Stoic Philosopher)

Being an *optimist* means that you neglect the negative side of things which can bite you in the butt. Being a *pessimist* means that you neglect the positive side of things which makes you unhappy and unmotivated because you are constantly worrying about what could happen. The *realist* sees both sides and deals with them equally. Realism is much more a conscious act where optimism and pessimism are more subconsciously.

Applying negative visualization will make you more realistic and happier and better prepared for possible problems. Applying positive visualization will make you more goal oriented and motivated.

Don't compare yourself to other people. Only compare your situation to all the possible positive and negative outcomes that a particular situation might have for you.

Here is how you perform negative visualization to be more confident, productive and successful:

- Imagine that your goal or project will fail spectacularly.

- Visualize all the possible causes of that failure and write them down one by one.

- Check the list and make sure that it is complete. Pay special attention to all the psychological causes why your goal or project might have failed.

- Make sure that the list is specific and realistic.

- Take your list of causes and rank each cause in such a way that you have the cause with the greatest impact and most likely threat on top and the cause with the least impact and least likely threat at the bottom.

- Start with the top 3 causes and brainstorm solutions to prevent the cause of failure to happen.

- Make an action plan for each of the solutions and make sure that these actions are written down specifically enough, measurable, realistic and that they have a planning and a deadline

- Visualize for each of the causes of failure how you will react appropriately in case they might occur.

By facing everything that can go wrong in case Murphy's Law comes in action, you will be much better prepared and therefore much more productive and successful.

Anti-Procrastination Hack:

Use Negative Visualization to reduce your fear of failure, fear of success, and fear of the unknown. Practicing Negative Visualization will boost your confidence, productivity, success, and happiness.

Don't be fooled by the tip of the iceberg

In the 19th century, a guy named Russell Conwell developed a famous speech he gave around 6,000 times. The speech was called Acres of Diamonds. The story is about an African farmer who had heard tales about other settlers who had made millions by discovering diamond mines. He was so excited about these tales that he wanted to find such a diamond mine himself. So, the farmer sold his farm and spent the rest of his life wandering the vast African continent, very unsuccessful, unfortunately. Finally, he threw himself into a river, broke and desperately.

Meanwhile, the man who had bought his farm, one day found a large, unusual stone in the stream which cut through the property. The stone turned out to be a diamond of enormous value. The new owner discovered that the farm was covered with much more of those stones and it was to become one of the world's richest diamond mines. The first farmer had owned acres of diamonds literally, but he sold them for practically nothing to look for them elsewhere. If he had first taken the time to study and prepare to learn what diamonds looked like in their rough state and explored his own land first, he would have found millions on his own property.

According to dr. Conwell, each of us is at this very moment standing in the middle of his own acres of diamonds if only we would have the wisdom and patience to intelligently and effectively explore the work in which we are now engaged. Because then we will usually find that it contains the riches we seek whether they are tangible or intangible. So, stop running from one thing to another forever looking for the pot of gold at the end of the rainbow and never staying with one thing long enough to find it. This is one of the reasons you always know, understand and acknowledge your Current Situation first.

If you look at successful people, you only see the times when they had success. That's the tip of the iceberg. But what you don't see is the thousands of hours that they have put in like an endless effort to improve their skills. You also don't see the endless obstacles they had to overcome to finally achieve success. If you only look at the tip of the iceberg, then you have a Procrastination Mindset. If you realize that the iceberg is much bigger than that and that it takes a huge amount of effort to get results, then you have an Anti-Procrastination Mindset. So, don't be intimidated by the success of others, because they too have put in the hard work. And if you only look at that success, you are limiting yourself. You too are able to put in the hard work as long as you focus on it so that you too can achieve success.

You have probably done your bookkeeping or administration before. Or if you have to lose weight or exercise, you probably have done that before as well. But you also have goals on which you have not worked before. For example, you see someone singing on TV, and you think "Hey, I want that too!" Or you see someone paragliding, and you think "Hey, that's what I want!" Or you see an author reading aloud from his own work, and you think "Hey, I also want to write a book!"

The only thing you see at that moment is the success. You see the tip of the iceberg. What you don't see, is all those years of training, practice and hard work that were needed to achieve the end-result that you see now. The success is visible, but all underlying processes and complexities are not visible. But because you've never done paragliding in your life before, you obviously have no idea what's involved. You just don't know that. Just like you also don't know what it takes to write a book. You don't know that because you've never done it before.

You can't see all of that from ignorance. The only thing you know is what you see, namely the end-result. And that looks very nice and promising. As a result of your short-sighted thinking, you can easily draw the wrong conclusion. That's why you only think "Hey, I want that too! I also want to be a chess grandmaster. Or I want to be good in X. "

But as soon as you start your new adventure, you soon discover that it is not all that simple. Things require a lot more time and are much more complex than you initially thought. That is the largest piece of the iceberg which is invisible. And the chances are that you get disappointed because it is not all that easy. And you are frustrated and want to give up. And that's something you don't want, so don't let yourself fooled by the tip of the iceberg.

Realize that there is a law of nature that says that behind every success, an incredibly large and complex world is hidden which you don't see.

Be realistic and realize that everything always costs more work and is more difficult than you think right now. Always keep in mind that things take twice as much time and money than you think beforehand. Then it can only get better.

Someone has just built their own house. Instead of immediately thinking "Hey, that's what I want!" Realize how much work, time and money will be involved in such a project. Is that something you are prepared to pay? Check that first.

Anti-Procrastination Hack:

Protect yourself from being blinded by the tip of the iceberg by realizing that there is a law of nature that says that behind every success, an incredibly large and complex world is hidden which you don't see.

Your Future-Self wants You to be a Goal-Getter right now

Future-self visualization, thinking constructively about your Future-Self, is one of the most powerful concepts I've come across in my years of studying the human mind and its impact on your success. Your Future-Self is all about you at some point in the future. Your future-self might be you in the very far or in the very near future. This depends on the goal you have with your future-self visualization. Your Future-Self is not an optimistic version of your future. Future-self visualization is also not the same as wishful thinking or a sort of dreamed state of you in the future. And it is also not a pessimistic version of where you are headed. No, your future-self is as realistic as you can make it. Find out the power of future-self visualization to help you challenge your procrastination temptation. Learn the 10 principles you need to take care of to become a real goal getter:

What is Future-Self Visualization?

The goal of future-self visualization is to define your future-self, based on your current-self and the goals you have. This is a harder task than you would think because most of us tend to think too optimistic about our future. All good will be better, and all the bad things will improve, you might think. But at the same time, you know that life is very unpredictable and that nothing goes in a straight line. So, when defining your future-self, you need to be realistic. Not optimistic, not pessimistic, but realistic. I know, taking a realistic view of your future-self can be painful, and you don't want to see your future-self which isn't bright, right? But does that mean you have to shut your eyes to it? No, of course not! Already the Roman emperors used to visualize their future-self, and they applied a special technique called negative visualization. This way of thinking is called Stoicism and much of the successful people of today still use this daily. So, why shouldn't you apply future-self visualization in the right way for yourself today? It will turn you from a procrastinator into a goal getter.

Your Future-Self wants you to be a Goal Getter

Now let's pick one of your goals. Step into your imaginary time travel machine and go to some point in the future. Depending on your goals, this might be in the near or far future. If your goal is to have the best holiday yet, then it will probably be soon. But if your goal is to develop a set of new skills and grow into a new career then it might take a few years.

Land yourself in your future and ask yourself how your future-self looks like:

- How will your future-self looks like?

- What about your future-self is remarkable?

- Are you happy with how your future-self looks like?

250

- What are you missing?
- What goals do your future-self have?
- How is your significant other reacting to your future-self?
- How are your family, friends, and colleagues reacting to your future-self?

Your Future-self acts as a resource for you. You can connect with it whenever you want, and it will serve as an internal source of motivation for you. Your Future-self will give you the motivation and inspiration you need to stay focused on your goals. Whenever you are stuck, just think of your future-self, and it will help you get through that difficult moment by giving you your focus on your goals back.

You can activate your future-self simply by visualizing a future situation. Did you know that everything which happens in your world, your outside world, first was imagined in your inside world? Your brain can't tell the difference between what is imagined and what is real. Your subconscious mind will always say "Yes!" to whatever you tell it. According to neuroscience the process of visualizing ideas in your head create the same biochemical reactions and feelings in your brain as if you were to have experienced it in real life already. So, when you do future-self visualization, your subconscious mind will get a memory of the new experience.

This will do two important things for you:

Future-self visualization will **create an Aha moment.** When you start to experience your new future-self, it will feel like as if you have experienced it before which makes the experience easier. Do you remember the story about the pilots Sully Sullenberger and Jeff Skiles? They had never experienced a plane crash before, but now that they did, it felt like an aha-moment because they had exactly visualized what to do when a plane crashes many times before.

Have you ever have had the experience of an Aha moment? Did you notice that you felt acquainted with something you thought was a brand-new experience? Well, probably you had imagined this experience earlier in your life already. Maybe not the exactly the same experience and with all the exact same details but something similar and more abstract. And perhaps you have already consciously forgotten that you had imagined this. But your subconscious mind has stored this imagination somewhere in your brain, and now these neural pathways are again triggered but now with a real-life situation. And while you trigger neural pathways which are already formed in one way or another, it feels acquainted for you, as if you have experienced it already: an Aha moment!

Furthermore, future-self visualization will **open up your eyes to see opportunities and possibilitie**s towards your future-self which you wouldn't have seen otherwise. If you are not expecting something, then often you also will not see it. How often have you looked for your keys or your phone but couldn't find it, while they lay right in front of your eyes? You weren't expecting it there! You know what they say: if you want to hide something, then hide it in plain sight, because no one will expect it there. The technical term for this is myopia or the quality of being short-sighted. This bias makes you blind to opportunities and possibilities to bring you towards your goals. This is a pity. But what if you could bypass your myopia? All kinds of opportunities and possibilities would suddenly come to your attention. The way to bypass your myopia is by doing future-self visualization. This will open up your mental filters to see the things necessary to accomplish your goals.

How Future-Self Visualization will help you to become a Goal Getter

When you start to use future-self visualization, you will learn to see the effects of the life of your current-self, projected into the life of your future-self. The decisions you make today have a long-term impact on your future-self. For example, if I eat too much and workout too little then probably I will gain some weight. If I don't think of my future-self at all, then I will not see and feel the impact of my decision to eat too much and workout too little. Instead, I will only see the short-term benefits and keep on doing it. When you use future-self visualization, you will be able to see and feel your future-self in one year from now, ten years from now, twenty years from now and so on. And then you can check for yourself whether you are happy with what you see or not. So, next time you are procrastinating on exercising, for example, perform a quick future-self visualization. Check how your future-self thinks about postponing your exercises. The chances are that your future-self will motivate you to go to the gym anyway.

Anti-Procrastination Hack:

Let your future-self motivate you to perform the tasks you have to do. Just visualize your future-self and how he will feel about doing or not doing the task.

Sometimes, you are not clear about your goals. For example, if you hear friends speaking about skiing, you can get overly enthusiastic about skiing yourself. Immediately, you say to them that you also want to ski. You take action immediately and start taking skiing lessons once per week. After a couple of weeks, you find it harder and harder to get yourself to the skiing lessons, and you start skipping once or twice. Soon, after that, you get a lousy feeling about yourself because you can't follow through. But you never checked if skiing is the right goal for you. You have so much else on your plate right now that skiing is the least important priority. You better spend your time on more important things. But while you decided to go skiing on an impulse, you don't know that. If you would have checked with your future-self, however, you would have known that skiing is not a good thing to do right now in your life. But unfortunately, you didn't. So, now you have wasted a lot of your time, energy and resources on chasing the wrong goal. And as a bonus, you think lousy of yourself, and you think that you are a procrastinator. This lowers your self-esteem, and you begin to procrastinate in other areas of your life as well. Do you get the picture?

Do yourself a favor, and always check whether you are pursuing the right goals or not by doing future-self visualization.

Anti-Procrastination Hack:

Check with your future-self whether or not your goals are appropriate for you to work on or not.

When you are pursuing your goals, you get distracted by all kinds of distractions every day. Your job is to stay focused on your goals and dreams until you have successfully achieved them. Future-self visualization will help you focus on your goals because you see the positive benefits from achieving your goals in the life of your future-self. This will give you the motivation to neglect distractions and to stay focused. I use future-self visualization every day to visualize how my life will look like in a few years' time in the context of the goals I'm working on. This is one of the first things I do when I wake up. Then during the day, I have enough motivation to stay focused. Sure, I am also distracted all the time. But the trick is to re-focus as soon as possible by reminding yourself why you are doing what you do in the first place. Future-self visualization will give your everyday actions a bigger purpose. It awakens the "real stonecutter" in you.

Anti-Procrastination Hack:

Give your daily actions a bigger purpose to help you motivate to do the tasks you need to do and become a goal getter.

Obstacles, setbacks, and disappointments in your life are a fact of life, but most of the time you don't see them coming. If you would perform future-self visualization, then you can apply negative visualization to see as many of the obstacles you will find on your path towards your future-self and already start to find solutions for them. And even better, find ways to prevent those barriers from happening. And even when obstacles are inevitable, you will not be surprised or depressed about them, but instead immediately put your plan B, C, D or .... Z into practice. So, instead of only using positive visualization also dare to look into the dark side of your future-self and find out whatever can go wrong. Then find ways to either avoid them or deal with them successfully when they are inevitable. If you want to go to the gym every day to get in better shape, then visualize how you will do that. See, how your alarm clock is waking you up at 05:30 in the morning. Are you happily jumping out of your bed, energized to go to the gym? Or are you a bit grumpy and still tired and do you want to turn back to bed immediately? Both scenarios can happen, you know. As well as every other scenario. So, how will you deal with the negative scenarios if they become a reality? Do you have a plan B ready? If you want to become a goal getter and leave procrastination behind you, you should start to visualize your future-self and make yourself resilient against possible negative scenarios.

108

Anti-Procrastination Hack:

Deal with setbacks upfront adequately so that they don't stand between you and your goal. Use future-self visualization to develop

> *counter scenarios for future setbacks.*

As you have read in a previous chapter, an Anti-Procrastination Mindset is very important for you to become a highly productive goal getter who has defeated his procrastination. Visualizing your future-self on a regular basis will enhance this Mindset. If you see your future-self, or even better, multiple versions of your future-self, then you will become aware of the fact that you can shape your future. This will strengthen your Anti-Procrastination Mindset which will make you more productive, successful and happy. A dear friend of mine, Joe, has all kinds of setbacks going on in his life. And whenever I think that he cannot sink lower, he gets another setback. But every time he seems to get accustomed to his new situation very quickly. Every time he settles for less. Unfortunately, he does not understand that he too can grow. Wherever you are in life, you always can grow. If Joe would visualize his future-self, then he would be able to respond to that in his current life, which would make him more responsible. So, don't be like Joe and strengthen your Anti-Procrastination Mindset by using future-self visualization.

109

Anti-Procrastination Hack:

Strengthen your Anti-Procrastination Mindset and become a highly productive goal getter by visualizing

> *your future-self regularly and seeing your potential to grow and develop yourself.*

So, how exactly do you do that? How do you visualize your future-self so that you become a goal-getter? Let's see ...

How to become a Goal-Getter by Visualizing your Future-Self

When doing future-self visualization, you need to alter your associated state of awareness with your dissociated state of awareness.

An **associated state of consciousness** is where you be your future-self. You look through your own eyes to your future situation. You will see what you will see when you have arrived in the future. You will hear what you will hear, and you will feel how you then will feel and so on.

The advantage of this associated state of awareness is that you will experience your future-self in the way what then will be the reality of your life. This gives you a chance to exactly notice how your life will be like. You will know if you are on the right track or not. If yes, then your current goals, decisions, and way of performing are good, and you don't have to change anything. If not, then you need to investigate what fails in your future situation and what you need to change today so that your future will change for the better.

The *disadvantage* of future-self visualization via an **associated state of awareness** is that your subconscious mind will think that this future state is already a reality. This means that there is no urge for your subconscious mind to do anything different or new because it thinks that your new reality has already become a reality. This is the perfect recipe for procrastination, and exactly that is what we don't want!!

That's why you also need to do your future-self visualization via a **dissociated state of awareness**. This means that when you visualize your future-self, you don't look through your own eyes to see your future situation. Instead, you see yourself in the picture. So, you see how your future-self will look like (a bit older probably) and you see what your future-self is doing and how your future-self is behaving in this future situation. It is as if you are in your own cinema watching a movie of your future life with you as the main character in it.

The *advantage* of this **dissociated state of awareness** is that your subconscious mind will now do everything to make this movie into a reality for you. Your subconscious mind will set all its filters in the direction of your future-self. It will motivate you to do whatever is necessary to achieve your future reality. This is motivating you on the one hand and killing your procrastination on the other! So, what are you waiting for? Start immediately with visualizing your future-self where you alternate between an associated and dissociated state of awareness.

110

Anti-Procrastination Hack:

Alternate your associated state of awareness with a dissociated state of awareness when doing future-self visualization. This will motivate you to do the work and will kill your procrastination.

As John Donne has said, "No man is an island." The same applies to goals: No Goal is an Island.

If you want to lose 10 pounds, then this goal has implications for all the people around you and all your other goals as well. For example, if this losing-10-pounds goal means that you need to work out 1 hour every day then you cannot spend that 1 hour on pursuing your other goals. In the long run, this can be a problem, because if your other goals are even important or more important than your goal of losing ten pounds, then you probably will find yourself ending up doing other things then working out. You probably will find yourself procrastinating on going to the gym and in the end, you might find yourself a loser for not achieving your goal. But in this case, not achieving your goal is not due to your lack of perseverance or due to your procrastination habit. It is just a matter of conflicting goals. So, before you start working on your goal, you need to think strategically first. You need to perform an ecology check. Use future-self visualization to check what the impact of achieving your goal is on the people around you. How will they react? Do they like your future-self in the way you want them to be? Or not? And what about the other areas of your life? Are they balanced and also reaping the benefits of your future-self?

The ultimate question when performing an ecology check on your future-self is asking yourself if your future-self in your visualization is the best version for yourself, for your goals, for the people around you and ultimately for the world. If you can answer this question with yes, then you are good to go. If not, then you know that you need to change something.

Anti-Procrastination Hack:

Use future-self visualization to perform an ecology check on your goals to make sure that you are working on the right goals and that they don't conflict with your other goals or the people around you. Only

> *then, you will be sure that your goal is feasible and that you have the chance to see it through until it is complete.*

One of the most powerful statements you can use to motivate yourself are statements starting with "I am ...." If you are using an "I am" statement, you tap into the source of your identity which is one of the most subconscious levels but nevertheless one of the most powerful. If you find yourself procrastinating on doing your administrative work, for example, the chances are that you think of yourself as a lousy administrator. To stop your procrastination, you can turn this around. Just say to yourself "I am a very good administrator." Your I-am's should be stated in a positive way oriented towards your goal. Now, also visualize yourself being a very good administrator and while you visualize that also say it to yourself.

Ask yourself: How do I want to be? And after you've answered that: Who do I want to be? Now formulate the answer to this question in the form of an I-am-statement: I am ...

You will see that your I-am's become stable and robust over time. For an I am like "I am slim, healthy, and fit" it doesn't matter if your goal is to lose 10 pounds or 20 pounds or that your goal is to work out more.

So, start with your I am's and say to yourself in your future-self visualization: "I am slim" while picturing an image of your future-self, being slim, "I am a very good administrator" while picturing an image of your future-self being a very good administrator.

Anti-Procrastination Hack:

Use "I am ..." statements to stop yourself from procrastinating so that you will tap into the power of your identity. Combine your "I am ..." statements with future-self visualization.

Involve your Subconscious Mind while visualizing your Future-Self

Visualizing your goals is cooperation between your subconscious mind and your conscious mind. They need to communicate and work together which is only possible if you can clear your conscious mind first. If your conscious mind is occupied with all kinds of worries, frustrations or other thoughts, it has no space left for input from the subconscious mind. This means that you will be distracted in the first few seconds of your visualization already. This is why it will help you if you start with a relaxed state of mind. A relaxed state of mind is a situation where your conscious mind will really listen to what your subconscious mind has to say to you. Remember that your conscious mind can only hold seven plus or minus two thoughts at the same time, so you are heavily dependent on your subconscious mind to guide you to the rich world of both your current-self and your future-self.

Did you know that apart from being awake and being asleep there are three other states of mind you can be in?

Your brain consists of billions of neurons. Those neurons need electricity to communicate with each other. As soon as your synapses are firing in synchrony, a neural network is created. This neural network is linked to a specific thought, memory, state of consciousness, or any mood or feeling. Have you ever said to anyone "I have a brainwave"? Well, that's the moment where this neural network is being activated. Like every wave in nature, a brain wave is cyclic. If you would attach yourself to an Electro Encephalo Gram (EEG) device, you would actually see those brain waves on the monitor.

Brain waves can be divided into five different bandwidths. Each bandwidth stands for a spectrum of human consciousness. See the infographic below, which you can download, if you'd like, for free together with all the other book bonuses.

Please, use the QR-code on page iv of this book to download them.

Alternatively, you could browse to:

https://SmartLeadershipHut.com/tapm-bonus

and download them!

During your deepest sleep, your brain produces Delta waves. Delta waves lie between 0.3Hz and 4Hz.

If you are meditating and you arrive in a very deep state, then your brain produces Theta waves. They lie between 4Hz and 8Hz.

When doing a typical kind of meditation or visualization, your brain produces Alpha waves. They lie between 9Hz and 13Hz. When your brain produces alpha waves, you are in an alpha state of mind. This state is being held responsible for being creative, coming up with new ideas.

When you are awake and in your regular daily routine at home or work, then your brain produces Beta waves. Beta waves lie between 14Hz and 30Hz. When your brain produces beta waves, you are in a beta state of mind. This means that you are alert, attentive, focused, engaged in decision making or problem-solving.

And if you are hyper-aware and in a higher state of conscious perception, your brain produces Gamma waves. Gamma waves lie between 25Hz and 100Hz. When in a Gamma state of mind, you can process information from different brain areas.

Especially alpha waves are very beneficial for you. An alpha state of mind makes you very present in the now. It relaxes your brain in a very calm state which gives you the opportunity to be alert and calm at the same time. Alpha waves improve the communication between all areas of your brain and also improve the mind-body connection. So, this is the state of mind you want to be in when performing visualization in general and future-self visualization in particular.

But how do you transition yourself from the normal Beta state of mind into the Alpha state of mind? Here is how:

Pick a place where you can sit quietly and where you will not be disturbed. Take a few deep breaths. Breathe in on the count of four and breathe out on the count of 8. Repeat this a couple of times. To help you even further to go into the alpha state of mind, I suggest you play a particular kind of relaxing background music. You can download this Stay Focused Music Bundle for free in the book bonus section for this book.

To train your mind to go into this alpha state of mind even quicker, it will help you to do this kind of visualization at the same time and place every day. Your subconscious mind is eager to react in the same way to the same triggers.

Now, you are ready to start your future-self visualization.

Anti-Procrastination Hack:

Make sure that the communication between your conscious and subconscious mind is optimal by bringing your mind into a relaxed state.

We all live a hectic life with too many accountabilities. Life can get in the way very easily. Your attention is needed for an urgent matter, so you postpone your planned activity until tomorrow. But you know that tomorrow never comes! Unless ... you make it a daily habit of visualizing your future-self. Now you will be reminded every day what your priorities are to work on. Furthermore, your mental filters and subconscious mind will be programmed for success with the continuous repetition over time.

Just follow these three steps:

1. Decide on your top 3 priorities for the coming weeks.

2. Choose a fixed time in your day, preferably immediately when you wake up.

3. Perform future-self visualization for each of the 3 goals every day on the chosen time until you have completed your goals.

Anti-Procrastination Hack:

Make future-self visualization a daily habit, so your priorities will always be on top of your mind.

When doing your future-self visualization, make sure that you use all your senses to make the picture as rich as possible. If you only say to yourself "I am slim" then you activate only the least powerful area of your brain. Instead, see yourself as slim, hear what you would hear when you are slim, feel what you then would feel, taste what you would taste and smell what you would smell. By activating all your senses in your visualization, you will activate and engage your whole brain; left and right, front and back. This will create all kinds of new neural pathways which will create Aha moments in your daily life supporting you to pursue your goal.

Anti-Procrastination Hack:

Make your visualization as rich as possible and incorporate all your senses. This activates and engages your whole brain.

The Secret Sauce for making your Intentions Stick

By now, you have learned how to develop the right Anti-Procrastination Mindset by balancing your Results-thinking with your Process-thinking in the right way. You have also learned how to plan and evaluate your day, week, month, year and life. Now, it comes all down to implementing everything you have learned. You have to develop a never say die attitude because you won't succeed in one straight line. You will get knocked down by life but after that immediately stand up. That's how you develop yourself into a goal getter. And to support you with that, I have a secret sauce which will motivate you all the way through to your success. It's called Positive Affirmations.

Positive Affirmations can be powerful if you know Why they work so well and How you should use them to your advantage. And that's precisely the topic of this chapter. We are going to explore why positive affirmations work so well to beat your procrastination and to help you become a goal getter.

The concept of positive affirmations already exists for ages. They were first popularized by French psychologist Emile Coué back in the 1920s. Also in that period, 1925, an actress, artist, and writer with the name Florence Scovel-Shinn published a famous book on success and affirmations. One of her affirmations were: "I have wonderful work in a wonderful way. I work very few hours for lots of pay."

Also Napoleon Hill, in his famous book Think and Grow Rich, speaks about positive affirmations. When Louise Hayes had written a book about positive affirmations in the 1970's, they became popular. And nowadays you can see positive affirmations all over the internet on Facebook, Instagram, Pinterest or Twitter posts. As everyone says, you need to repeat those positive affirmations, and they will change your life. But do they?

I have read Hayes' book already in the early 1980's and used them a lot. But have I seen the difference? Has the use of positive affirmations had a positive impact on my life? Let's find out:

What are Positive Affirmations?

Forty plus years or something after Hayes' book, there is a lot of scientifical research done to backup up the power of positive affirmations. The general conclusion about positive affirmations is that it can improve your mind and body. So, let's have a look at what exactly positive affirmations are, how positive affirmations work and what the best practices are for you to leverage the power of positive affirmations in your way.

If you only have seen positive affirmations but never have used them yourself, you might think that positive affirmations are just feel good quotes or positive statements. But they are so much more than that.

Positive affirmations are statements stated in a positive way that is repeatedly spoken to encourage the person speaking them and uplift him or her. Positive affirmations are like the language of your brain, and they follow a particular formula.

Your brain, especially your subconscious mind, follow specific rules when it comes to positive affirmations. This is why you cannot blindly use a positive affirmation you find somewhere on the internet.

Your subconscious mind will not recognize the affirmation accurately if you don't follow these 3 rules:

1) State positive affirmations in the present tense

Your brain only responds to statements in the present tense. So, instead of saying "I will be slim," say: "I am slim." Do you see the difference? And by the way: do you Feel the difference?

Let's try it again.

Say to yourself, while looking in the mirror: "I will be slim." How does that feel? Does that motivate you?

Now say, while looking into the mirror: "I am slim." How does that feel? Does that motivate you?

The last statement is probably much more enticing for you than the first one, isn't it? This is because if a statement is in the future tense, then it will not appeal to you as much as if the statement would be in the present tense.

2) Positive affirmations should only include positive words and no negative words

Your subconscious mind is not able to process negatives. You can try it for yourself. Observe what will happen in your head, when you read the following:

"Do not think, I repeat, do not think of a pink elephant!"

What happened in your mind right now? Did you see a picture of a pink elephant coming by? Exactly! That's because your subconscious mind has to grasp the meaning of a pink elephant first before it can say: "Oh oh, I shall not think about that!". But then what? If your subconscious mind is not allowed to think about a pink elephant, what should it think about? It does not know!! So, the chances are that it will automatically be pulled back to the picture of the pink elephant thus strengthening all the neural pathways in your brain connected with that picture.

Do yourself a favor and be very direct and specific about what it is that you want your subconscious mind to think about. For example: "Think of a blue elephant."

3) Speak your positive affirmations out loud as if they are already a fact or the truth

This means two things.

First of all, you need to develop powerful statements which sound like a fact. So, instead of saying "Maybe I am slim," say: "I am slim."

Secondly, use appropriate body language and tone of voice to state this positive affirmation as truth.

State the affirmation out loud as if you are entirely convinced of what you are saying.

Anti-Procrastination Hack:

Follow the three rules for crafting exciting, compelling and motivating positive affirmations which have the power to help you get your stuff done and finally achieve some results.

Why do Positive Affirmations work?

To understand why positive affirmations work, let's first have a look at how your brain works. Like any tool, the same applies to your brain: the better you understand the tool, the better you can work with it.

Your brain consists literally of trillions of synapses, and every little piece of information is stored by making neural connections between those synapses. Your brain is active 24/7, always sending and receiving instructions and thoughts at the speed of light.

As soon as you want to lift a finger, a complicated and complex construct of neural pathways are triggered through your nervous system to give your finger-muscles exactly the right instructions. I don't know how, but scientists have calculated that our brain processes millions of bits of information every second of the day. And this is done all in a very literal way.

An instruction is an instruction. Nothing more and nothing less.

But our conscious mind is only capable of processing 7 plus or minus 2 chunks of information at the same time. That's why our subconscious mind works for 95% of the time on autopilot, processing all those millions of bits of information.

This is a good thing because this frees up mental capacity for your conscious mind to do the strategic thinking. But it can also become a problem when your subconscious mind processes information in a way which doesn't suit your goals anymore. This process is called **mental filtering**, and it is done by your reticular activating system (RAS). The enormous amount of information to be processed is filtered by your subconscious mind. Only a minimal residue will ever reach your conscious mind. Most of the time in a distorted way.

If you don't consciously decide yourself, your subconscious mind will do it for you.

How many objects do you have in your living room? If you have a living room like most people, then you probably can easily count a hundred different objects. But when was the last time you really observed and experienced every single object? Probably a long time ago, because while all those objects are already for so long in your living room, you take them for granted. You don't really see them anymore, consciously. That's because your subconscious mind filters out all that unnecessary information. If you would consciously observe every one of the 100 objects every time you enter your living room, then you would not have much time left for more important things.

But what if one of those objects in your living room needs your attention? It might be that it needs to be dusted, or that it needs to be repaired. It will never get your attention because your subconscious mind is continuously filtering it out for you. This is when your autopilot brain is hindering you instead of helping you.

This was just a simple example of course, but it works the same for when you want to achieve your goals.

See your subconscious mind as millions of employees in your company. You are the CEO of course. You give department A with 10,000 employees the target to get you in shape. But now you as the CEO are going to do something else. Your attention moves to other parts of your company. What will happen with department A, do you think? Sure, they will work very hard for you, and they will do their utmost to get you in shape. On your path to achieving that goal, tens or hundreds of decisions need to be taken. And they will take these decisions without consulting you. Where do you think that will end up? Exactly on the same spot, you intended? Of course not! Every decision your subconscious mind takes on autopilot will probably deviate from your goal and your expectations. That's why good CEO's always keep communicating the overall goals and company values to all of their employees. And that's precisely the power of positive affirmations!

Positive affirmations will program your subconscious mind exactly to do what you want it to do because it is continuously reminded of your goals and what's important to you. Furthermore, positive affirmations will align all departments of your subconscious mind to work together towards your goals. As a span of horses, your subconscious mind will be much more effective when all forces are pointed in the right direction instead of being scattered around all over the place. That's the difference between a focused mind and a distracted mind. When you meet challenges on your path to your goal, and they will come(!), then you need the resilience to push through this resistance, so that you will be successful in achieving your goal. Strengthening the neural pathways necessary for your goal will help you get that resilience. And this is done by using positive affirmations.

Anti-Procrastination Hack:

Use Positive Affirmations to beat your procrastination temptation and to take control of your subconscious mind.

The illusion of time for your brain

My dog Bella does not know what the difference is between now and the past or the future. If I say to her "No Bella, you don't get your food right now; you will get your food in an hour," then she is all waggling with her tail and enthusiastically spinning around me because she thinks that she gets food immediately.

This is exactly how your brain also operates. As soon as you use the word "food," a series of neural pathways are fired off in your brain. And you cannot stop that. As well as the brain can't process negatives, it also can't process time.

So, the following sentences:

- I am slim
- I was slim
- I will be slim
- I am not slim

will all trigger neural pathways connected with the word slim. However, ... with the latter 3 sentences, your brain will be confused and will burn its mental energy for nothing. Only with the first sentence, your brain exactly knows what to do.

So, be aware of what you are saying to yourself and how you are saying it. Each word you use will trigger an internal representation in your brain.

Let's look at another example:

You have to give an important presentation next week. But as soon as you think about it, right now, you get nervous. Why is that? The thought of this presentation fires off all kinds of neural pathways right now. And apparently, these neural pathways in your brain are attached to other pathways with the feeling of nervousness. So, although you are sitting on your couch in a very comfortable and safe situation, your heart is pounding because you feel nervous! That's because your brain can't distinguish the now from the future. There is only now. So, when you think about something which will happen in the future, you will experience it right now.

So, do yourself a favor and state your positive affirmations in the present tense, since this is the only form your brain can process. And the less mental energy it will cost your brain to process your instructions, the more chance that the right and only the right neural pathways are being triggered. It's all a matter of precision. If you want to become slimmer, then you need to exactly trigger those neural pathways which are associated with you being slim. And the best way to fire off these exact neural pathways is to give exact instructions to your brain: "I am slim."

Anti-Procrastination Hack:

Watch your language and choose your words wisely when you talk to yourself. The most effective way to communicate with yourself is to give yourself very precise instructions so that exactly the right neural networks in your brain are fired off without costing it you too much mental energy. If you want to achieve something, help yourself by stating it in the present tense and in a positive way.

Use Positive Affirmations to create a Paradigm Shift

When using positive affirmations, you might find yourself an imposter. Let's say that your positive affirmation is: "I weigh 120 pounds". But your actual weight is 140 pounds.

Every time you are delivering the positive affirmation to yourself, you might find it awkward and uncomfortable. You will feel the tension between your

Current-Self and your Future-Self. And this is exactly one of the purposes of using positive affirmations.

Only if you feel the tension of the discrepancy of your Current-Self with regards to your Future-Self, you will have a motivation to come into action and take action towards your goal.

Instead of quitting with positive affirmations, this is the time you need to pursue and to break through your internal resistance. So, pursue with delivering your positive affirmations at least once or twice a day and use the tension to get motivated to do the work which will get you towards your goals.

10 Rules for crafting the best possible positive affirmations that actually work for you

On the internet, you can find lots of lists with positive affirmations. But will they work for you?

In my opinion, it is best to craft a positive affirmation for yourself, tailor-made for the occasion you want the positive affirmation to use for.

But how do you craft the best possible positive affirmations that will work the best for you? Well, just follow these rules:

1) Use positive words in your affirmations

Positive words are words which are aimed towards your goal. Don't use words that are pushing you away from what you don't want.

So, if your goal is to become slim, don't say: "I don't want to be fat anymore" because that is giving you an internal representation of you being fat. You don't want this!

Instead, use a word which describes your goal: slim.

So, say: "I am slim."

2) Make your positive affirmations sound powerful

Instead of saying: "I hope that I will ace that interview," say: "I have aced that interview!" or, even better, "I ace every interview!"

Make the affirmation compelling. Say it out loud to yourself, and ask yourself if it excites you or not. Try out multiple versions and choose the one which excites you the most.

3) State your positive affirmations in the present tense

Instead of saying: "Next year I will be slim, hopefully," say: "I am slim now" even if you think you're not.

This also means that you don't want to put a date or so in your affirmation. Every date you use implies that it will be a future thing and not a now thing.

4) Make sure your positive affirmation is relevant to your situation and your goal

The more specific your affirmation will be towards your goal, the more chance that you will trigger the right neural pathways associated with your goal. This is the reason why you want to craft your own affirmations instead of using a general one you have found on the internet or in a book.

So, instead of saying "I am slim," say "I weigh 120 pounds" if that's your goal. Think about what it is that you want to achieve. And now imagine how it will look like if you have achieved your goal. What is the end result? Can you make the end result measurable?

When you have an upcoming job interview, and you want that to be the best interview you have ever had, think about what the end result will look like. Probably, you are working for the new company. So, imagine yourself working for the new company. Instead of saying "The interview will be great" say: "I am working for company XYZ because I am the best man for the job."

5) Repeat your affirmation as often as possible

The trick with positive affirmations is repetition. Every time, you repeat your affirmation, you train your brain for success. If your goal is a Long-Term Goal, then repeating your affirmation once or twice a day will be perfect. If your goal is a short-term goal, because it is about you giving a successful presentation tomorrow, then you better repeat the affirmation as much as possible today and tomorrow until you have successfully completed your presentation.

Rule of thumb is that you have to practice your positive affirmations at least once per day. Preferably immediately after you wake up.

6) Be fully focused when you deliver your positive affirmation to yourself

When you deliver your affirmation to yourself, make sure that you are entirely focused on it. Don't just say it. Mean it. Be fully aware of it. Feel it.

That's the best chance you have to trigger the right neural pathways in your brain. Otherwise, the power of your affirmation gets lost in a sea of other neural connections going on in your brain.

Don't watch television while you are delivering positive affirmations to yourself. Instead, look at yourself in the mirror and speak them out loud to yourself.

7) Empower your affirmation with the power of visualization

When using positive affirmations, you only use one of the six mental channels you have at your disposal: your auditive digital channel. This is your self-talk. Why not use all your six mental channels? So, also use your visual, auditive, kinesthetic, olfactory, and gustatory senses and your self-talk. The more mental channels you use, the more ingrained your goal get into your nervous system. So, visualize your goal. How will it look like when you have achieved your goal? What will you see and what will you not see? What will you hear? What will you feel and how will you feel? What will you smell? What will you taste? And what will you say to yourself? This last part is where your positive affirmation comes into practice. The benefit of using all of your senses is that it will be easier to feel that you have achieved your goal.

Think of your goal. Let's say that your goal is to give an excellent presentation tomorrow and that you get approval for your project proposal. How would you feel if this has become a reality? To create this feeling, you first have to visualize yourself giving an excellent presentation, and after that, you visualize the approval you get from your stakeholders. How will you walk, how will you talk, how will you feel when you have achieved this? Great!

That's the feeling you want to have now when delivering your positive affirmation: "I have given an excellent presentation and have gotten approval for my project proposal."

Having this feeling of success now will make it easier for your subconscious mind to find the right neural pathways associated with this achievement.

8) Make sure you are in a relaxed state of mind

Communication between your conscious mind and subconscious mind really only work when you are relaxed. And delivering positive affirmations is communicating with your subconscious mind.

So, when delivering positive affirmations, seek for a place where you can sit quietly without being disturbed. Take a few deep breaths and then deliver your positive affirmations to yourself.

9) Never mind "how"

If you deliver the positive affirmation "I have given an excellent presentation," don't start to question how on earth this will come true, because then you ruin the process. It is as if you plant the seeds for a beautiful tree and after a month start digging in the ground to see if the seeds have grown or not. That's ruining the process.

Let your subconscious mind do the job for you. See yourself as the CEO of a billion-dollar company with millions of employees. You have set the goals for each department. Now, it is their job to figure out how to achieve those goals.

It's your job to repeat the goals as long as necessary and see to it that they will deliver. And exactly that is what you do when you repeat your positive affirmations daily.

10) Take your positive affirmations for granted

Don't ask how, but also don't ask when. Trust the process. Like the seeds, you planted in the ground, the only thing you can do is trust the process. Trust nature to do its thing.

If you have crafted your positive affirmations the way I described in this chapter and if you deliver them daily the way described here, then you are good to go. The only thing you have to do is to trust your subconscious mind that it will do whatever it takes to help you achieve your goal.

One more thing you need to know about using positive affirmations

If you only use positive affirmations as a standalone tool, then chances are that they will not work for you. The reason is that positive affirmations only scratch the surface of your subconscious mind. Studies of the

University of Pennsylvania showed that in every communication, the power of words is only 7% whereas the power of your tone of voice has an impact of 38% and the power of your body language has an impact of 55%. In every communication. So, also in the communication between your conscious mind and your subconscious mind, it is important also to use body language and tone of voice.

Positive affirmations can help you with nearly every goal you want to accomplish in your life, even if the goal seems imaginable.

But, if you only use positive affirmations, this means that you leave out the most powerful tools you have in your communication which is your tone of voice and your body language. The best way to engage the latter two is to use also visualization and anchoring. If you use visualization together with positive affirmations, then you have a very powerful combination at your disposal. Furthermore, you need to pay attention to negative thoughts and beliefs when delivering your positive affirmations together with your visualization. Jane Fonda was held to be one of the most gorgeous women in the world. Yet, she herself thought otherwise, as her autobiography reveals. She struggled with eating disorders for decades due to her inadequate judgment of her physical appearance. What would have happened if Mrs. Fonda would have said in front of the mirror to herself: "I am beautiful." Well, probably she would feel disgusted with herself. This has everything to do with a belief conflict. This should have been a strong signal for her to turn her negative belief into a positive one.

So, if a positive affirmation is in conflict with a deep belief, then it will not work. Unless ... you are going to work to change that belief. This is how positive affirmations can help you too. By using positive affirmations, you can detect negative beliefs in yourself which will hinder you from achieving your goals and being successful. To be consciously aware of your negative beliefs is the first and most important step towards change. After that, you can work on yourself to turn the negative beliefs into positive ones. One of the ways to do that is by using visualization and positive affirmations but now tied to solving the negative belief.

For example, in the case of Jane Fonda, it might have been that, after having done some soul searching, she would have discovered that she had a strong negative belief that she is not worth the attention, that she is not worth it. Caused by this belief, she thought about herself as not beautiful enough and caused by that she had all kinds of eating disorders.

By stating the positive affirmation "I am beautiful" in front of the mirror, she would have discovered inner discrepancies. And after some soul searching, she would have discovered that this was fueled by her belief that she is not worth it.

To turn this negative belief around, she could have developed positive affirmations like "I am worth it! I am enough." while visualizing herself amidst a group of loving and caring people while just being enough and worth the attention. After practicing this kind of visualizations and positive affirmations for a couple of months, her belief system would have changed into "I am worth it!" and "I am enough!"

Now, when she would have returned to her original positive affirmation "I am beautiful" this would probably have felt natural and as a universal truth to her.

So, do you see how this works? Sometimes, we have a goal and use visualization and positive affirmations to re-program our mental filters towards that goal, and then it appears that there is on a deeper more subconscious level a negative belief which hinders us from achieving that goal. This is how positive affirmation will help you on a whole different level: to discover your self-sabotage mechanism which is the cause of your procrastination. The way to deal with this is like in the example with Jane Fonda. Just have patience with yourself and decide to solve the sabotage thing first by really listening to your subconscious mind.

Positive affirmations and Visualizations have the power to pull you out of your comfort zone because your subconscious mind experiences a visualization as a real-life situation. If your goal is to run the New York marathon in three months from now, while you have not moved your body for the last three years, then visualizing that you run this marathon, may scare you like hell! And that's a good thing! Because now you can do a reality check for yourself on the feasibility of your goal. And furthermore, you can dig deeper into your subconscious mind to discover which sabotage mechanisms you are hindering you from being a marathon runner. Now you have new short-term goals to work on first before you can plan your New York marathon.

Final Thoughts on How to Stop Procrastinating

YES!! You did it! You have reached the final chapter of this book! I congratulate you for that! Most people, including me, strand somewhere in the first chapters of a book without ever reaching the end of the book. But not you, though! Great work!

So, by now you know that Procrastination is something most of us cope with. So, there is nothing to be ashamed of. We didn't get a manual of our operating system when we were born. We also didn't get an education in proper thinking. But now you have. You now know that procrastination is just a matter of having the wrong mindset. And you have learned that it is very much possible to change your procrastination mindset into an anti-procrastination mindset. Develop your Results-thinking skills and your Process-thinking skills and balance both ways of thinking the right way and you will turn into a highly successful goal getter!

In this book, we have discussed a lot of thinking strategies. Just reading them is not enough. You have to practice them deliberately.

So, I urge you to overcome the resistance all readers have whenever they complete a book. In other words, instead of finishing this book, and moving on to the next title, I recommend implementing what you've just learned.

One of the best ways to start doing that is to schedule a couple of very important meeting in your agenda.

So, take your agenda, please.

Do it now!

Schedule a daily appointment with yourself where you apply Process-thinking. Preferably at the same time each day.

Schedule also a Weekly Review meeting where you apply Results-thinking and Process-thinking to review your weekly goals in comparison with your quarterly goals.

And finally, schedule a Quarterly Review meeting where you apply Results-thinking to review your quarterly goals in comparison to your Long-Term Goals. Furthermore, review if your Long-Term Goals are still on track or need slight adjustments.

During those daily, weekly and quarterly meetings, you will learn to apply and to train your anti-procrastination mindset.

Furthermore, I suggest that you use your Weekly Review meeting to check the list with Anti-Procrastination Hacks, see appendix. You will learn in next section, the appendix, how to optimally make use of these hacks.

Last but not least, I suggest becoming a member of our private VIP Facebook Group where we will hold each other accountable for implementing all the lessons and anti-procrastination hacks of this book. Every workday of the week, I will post one of the anti-procrastination hacks in our Facebook Group, for you as a continuous reminder. Also, you have the chance to share your personal experience implementing the anti-procrastination hacks on a day-to-day basis and ask questions to the group members or, even better, give other group members advice based on your own experience.

Always remember, that if you only optimize yourself with one percent each, you will be a whole new person next year! So, take baby steps, but consistently take them!

Until we meet in our Facebook Group,

Live Fully and Be Awesome!

Harry Heijligers

Appendix with the 117 Anti-Procrastination Hacks

All of the 117 Anti-Procrastination Hacks which have been described throughout this book are listed below. In the first column, you see a reference number. If you click on the link, you will be directed directly to the particular section in this book where the particular hack is discussed. There you will find why the hack is important, what exactly it is and how you should optimally deal with it.

My suggestion to you is this: after you have read the book once in its entirety, go over the list of Anti-Procrastination Hacks below. Choose just one hack you want to implement first. What's your weakest link, right now?

Pay attention to this one chosen hack for a day, or maybe a couple of days until you have implemented this hack in your life.

Remember, if you improve yourself with only one percent per day, you will be a totally different person in one year from now. So, just go steady over the hacks one by one and develop your consistency. As soon as you have implemented an anti-procrastination hack, mark it down in the third column. This will give you a feeling of completion which will release dopamine in your brain. This highly motivates you to keep optimizing yourself.

Please, download a free copy with all the hacks in the book bonuses section.. This way, you can print it out for yourself, which makes it easier to keep track of your progress.

Nr.	Anti-Procrastination Hack
001	Dare to make mistakes as quickly as possible and maximize your learnings.
002	Say to yourself: "I am excited to start this new task" instead of saying that you are nervous or afraid. Start using this positive affirmation: "I am always excited when I start something new!"
003	Put your urge to put things off on hold. Take a 10-minute break. A mental break! Not a distraction from social media or so! Meditate or take a walk. This gives your cold thinking a chance to step in. What will be the impact on your future-self?
004	Don't work on anything which is not adding up to a clear goal which excites you. Always start with defining a clear goal which excites you in all roles you play and on all levels.
005	To beat your procrastination, you need direction and focus. Follow along with successful people and schedule your daily strategic thinking time to create this direction and focus for yourself on a consistent basis.
006	Develop a clear vision of the end goal and keep this vision in your mind at all times. This makes you consistent over time.

Nr.	Anti-Procrastination Hack
007	Unknown is Unloved. Perform future-self visualization on a daily basis, so that you come to love your future-self and you no longer avoid cracking the hard nuts because you know and feel that it will harm your future-self.
008	To get you motivated to start your task, make the very first step as small as possible, so that you can't refuse to take it. Identify the tiniest little domino stone, that, when thrown over, will throw over everything else.
009	Fuel your internal motivation, by having a clear picture of the end result and how that will benefit you.
010	Break-down the task until you know exactly what to do and where to ask help for.
011	Don't procrastinate on boring tasks. Be aware that even boring tasks can add up to winning the Nobel Prize. Know your overall game plan and how small tasks are related to that. Without throwing off that first tiny little domino stone, nothing else will be accomplished.
012	Don't fall into the procrastination trap! Don't think that you have not enough time to spend on working on your goal. Even if you have only five minutes left on your agenda, it is better to do something tiny than nothing at all.
013	Take back control over your life! Get to know your reptilian brain and how to control it, instead of letting your reptile brain control you!

Nr.	Anti-Procrastination Hack
014	Use Visualization techniques to control your Reptilian Brain because your Reptilian Brain is highly visual.
015	Motivate your Reptilian Brain to focus on your goal, by focusing on avoiding pain first.
016	Learn to accept pain as something good, as something which ultimately brings you the pleasure. Expect the pain, endure the pain, resolve the pain.
017	Motivate yourself to do the things you need to do by checking what the pain is you can avoid by doing them.
018	Appeal to the self-centered nature of your Reptilian Brain. Answer the question: What's in it for me? Be certain that there is always something positive to find.
019	Use Contrast to demonstrate the importance of doing the task instead of procrastinating on it.
020	Make the task you need to perform as tangible as possible. Be creative and give the task a visual, kinesthetic or auditory representation.
021	Make a clear transition between the tasks you are working on. Especially the task you tend to procrastinate on, need to be distinguishable from the other tasks. For example, use different background music or change the scenery.
022	Mindset is everything. There is no building built, no victory won, and no world record is broken without the initial necessary spark that started in someone's mind.

Nr.	Anti-Procrastination Hack
023	Be aware that having a Procrastination Mindset makes it easy for you to procrastinate because you think that putting in the effort is useless anyway. Instead, adopt The Anti-Procrastination Mindset that will change your way of thinking from a procrastinator into a highly successful goal getter.
024	Be aware that your Procrastination Mindset is withholding you from being successful in every area of your life. Ditch it asap!
025	Start to develop an Anti-Procrastination Mindset. This will help you to change your way of thinking so that you will get more focus and clarity on your path to success and the drive to follow through on it.
026	Don't believe that your future is carved out in stone because it is not. Instead, your future is malleable. The big question for you is, if you want to shape your future yourself or that you let it shape by sheer randomness.
027	Never give up on your goals! Expect setbacks to come your way. Get up. Learn from them. Follow through on your goals until you have achieved them.
028	After you have set your goals, don't focus on them anymore. Instead, focus on the effort you need to put in to achieve your goals.

Nr.	Anti-Procrastination Hack
029	Be the cause of your results. You can't control your results. You only can control the efforts you take to get to the results. See the result you get only as a measure of the effectiveness of your efforts and nothing more than that. Learn from your results and if necessary, course correct. At all costs, do not let yourself down based on the results.
030	Take control over the effort you put in to achieve your goals. Evaluate after a period of time, how you have performed, based on the results you got. Use the results only to evaluate your previously made progress assumptions.
031	Be aware that complaining about a situation or blaming others is just an excuse to procrastinate. Stop it! Instead, ask yourself what you could do differently to get better results and course correct.
032	Don't expect results too quickly. It's unrealistic and counterproductive. It's a way to self-sabotage yourself. Instead, focus on the work which needs to be done and let go of your expectations of the result you will gain from that. Use the Visual Squash technique to help you with that.
033	Know, Understand and Acknowledge your Current Situation, so that you know for sure and with confidence what to do and where to start.
034	Results-thinking done properly has the power to motivate you to achieve your goals until successful.

Nr.	Anti-Procrastination Hack
035	Results-thinking done inappropriately will cause that you either procrastinate or give-up on your goal entirely. You will lose the motivation to overcome the inevitable obstacles on your way to your goal.
036	Develop a passion for your top five life purposes, so that you create rocket energy within you to relentlessly pursue your goals and so that even the most tedious tasks become enjoying.
037	Make sure you don't perform activities which are not necessary right now because this might cause you to procrastinate on things that are very important to do right now.
038	Use Process-thinking to prevent possible waiting times because this might cause you to procrastinate.
039	Use Process-thinking to prevent unnecessary movement or transport of things which might tempt you to procrastinate.
040	Use Results-thinking to avoid the trap of "gold plating your goal." Instead, make your goal realistic and achievable to avoid procrastinating on it.
041	Use Process-thinking to avoid unnecessary distractions and instead make you unstoppable in achieving your goals.
042	Balance Results-thinking with Process-thinking to continually course correct yourself on your way to achieving your goals.

Nr.	Anti-Procrastination Hack
043	Every Passion deserves to be fulfilled, but this becomes only true if you focus your passion with laser-precision. Use the 4-step process to decide on your top 5 goals for the coming years and say no to everything else.
044	Develop a passion for your top five life purposes, by using Vision Boards, Values, Future-Self Visualization, and Positive Affirmations.
045	Set your goals adequately so that you have the maximum chance of success. Your Long-Term Goals serve as your True North, and you don't want to throw away your energy and resources by driving yourself in the wrong direction. So, make sure your goals are challenging, clear and well-defined, have a deadline and are measurable.
046	The first step towards crafting your Long-Term Goals for your life is to choose an area in your life for which you want to develop your goals for.
047	The second step towards crafting your Long-Term Goals for your life is to brainstorm goals within a chosen life area.
048	The third step towards crafting your Long-Term Goals for your life is to choose the top 5 goals per life area.
049	The fourth step towards crafting your Long-Term Goals for your life is to make sure that they are well-defined so that you are set up for success.
050	The fifth step towards crafting your Long-Term Goals for your life is to write them down and give them a visual representation.

Nr.	Anti-Procrastination Hack
051	There is a fine line between giving up too quickly and chasing your dreams too long. The art of life is to balance that fine line in your advantage. You don't want to be a Don Quixote, but you also don't want to be a loser who never achieves anything. This is why you need to balance your Results-thinking with Process-thinking. This will give you a higher chance of making wise decisions to your advantage.
052	Use both Results-thinking and Process-thinking to get unstuck. Evaluate if you have dealt with obstacles effectively and efficiently and decide on ending the project you are working on or pursuing with it and dealing with the challenges. Either way, take a conscious decision.
053	To perform Results-thinking, use this two-step process: 1) Define the scope of your thinking; 2) Ask yourself the different questions within the chosen scope.
054	Define quarterly goals as a bridge between Results-thinking and Process-thinking to help you actually get results and stay on track.
055	Procrastination is a good thing as long as it concerns tasks which are not on your top 5 of priorities!
056	Use your Vision Board to improve your goal-setting and to help you visualize your goals.
057	Create your Vision Board in three phases: Preparation, Creation, and Manifestation to focus your mental energy and become a goal getter instead of a procrastinator.

Nr.	Anti-Procrastination Hack
058	Vision Boards are a powerful tool for you to gain focus and motivation to work on your short-term and Long-Term Goals. Your Vision Board will help you stay focused and motivated even when distractions and setbacks arise on your way to your goal (which is a fact of life). Let your Vision Board end your procrastination temptation!
059	Knowing your personal values will give you the inner peace to always know which decision to take. Above all, they will make you happier and more successful.
060	Define your values in the context of your Long-Term Goals to make sure your values are fully aligned with those goals.
061	To prepare yourself to explore your Personal Values, clear your mind first, focus your mind on one Long-Term Goal, and withhold your critical conscious mind from stepping in too soon.
062	Cut through the list of 500 personal values to create the first draft of your values in the context of your goal. Remember to focus your mind on this question while sieving through the list: "In the context of my Long-Term Goal X, what do I find important?"
063	Cut again through the list of values, you narrowed down in step 1. Create the second draft of your values in the context of your goal. Remember to focus your mind on this question while sieving through the list: "In the context of my Long-Term Goal X, what do I find important?"

Nr.	Anti-Procrastination Hack
064	Structure your Personal Values into a Values Hierarchy by chunking your values up and down.
065	Check your Values Hierarchy for completeness by asking yourself the Leave- and Stay-question.
066	Analyze whether or not your Values Hierarchy is supporting you for the full 100% in achieving your goal. For anything less than 100%, design your most optimal Values Hierarchy.
067	Use the two-step process to implement your optimized Values Hierarchy to support you in achieving your goal by using tools like a Vision Board, Visualization and Positive Affirmations.
068	Let your Values Hierarchy guide you through your day when deciding which activities are important enough to complete.
069	Don't procrastinate on the goals which are most important to you. Instead, learn to say No to competing projects by evaluating new ideas and initiatives before committing to them.
070	Plan your activities in sprints of 20 minutes. This makes it easy to fill small spaces of time left with doing something useful. It also makes starting an activity easier because it is manageable.
071	Schedule a fixed time every day to perform Process-thinking. Evaluate your past day, plan your coming day and have an outlook on the next seven days. Plan your tasks in chunks of 20-minutes to keep you motivated and to get stuff done.

Nr.	Anti-Procrastination Hack
072	Process-thinking gets stuff Done. It will take out your resistance against the activities you have to perform, and it will help you see the successful outcome of your activities. Less resistance and more motivation equal less procrastination and more stuff done.
073	Study every one of the 15 Process-thinking Strategies to help you get stuff Done.
074	Use Process-thinking to plan your weekly and daily tasks based on your quarterly goals. Make sure you visualize the very first step of each task for today so that starting that task will be very easy.
075	Put urgent matters into perspective and find the right balance in handling them immediately vs. not letting yourself be distracted.
076	Optimize yourself continuously by reviewing your productivity progress on a daily basis. Use the review questions to evaluate your day. If you are happy with your results, great! If not, optimize yourself by saying: "Needs work!"
077	When you plan your day, identify the top 3 most important tasks you want to accomplish. This should be your primary focus. Aim to do those tasks first thing in the morning, so that you will be energized to work on other things the rest of the day.
078	Spend your time only on activities which are important for you and your goals. Use the Eisenhower matrix easily to decide what you should work on and what not.

Nr.	Anti-Procrastination Hack
079	Do quick tasks which can be completed within a few minutes immediately or as soon as your current task is finished. Don't let procrastination become your invisible enemy!
080	Starting and completing complex, time-consuming, and annoying tasks is easy. Instead of focusing on the big and ugly domino stones, find that one little tiny domino stone which is easy to start and complete and which has the power to throw over all the other domino stones. Make starting the first and tiniest task your primary goal.
081	Use a tool like a fishbone diagram to break down your project into small bite-sized chunks which can be accomplished within one hour. Everything gets easier when you break it down.
082	Work, in short, intense sprints of 25 minutes on your task (Pomodoro technique). This helps you to beat your procrastination temptation and increases your focus.
083	See discomfort as a way to develop yourself and achieve your goals. Discomfort is your friend. Don't' shy away from it! Embrace it! It is the only way forward.
084	Dissociate yourself from your discomfort feeling. Focus your mind on something else. Focus your mind on the goals you want to achieve and the results you will reap from that. Write your feelings down and analyze them. Define your first bite-sized action step.

Nr.	Anti-Procrastination Hack
085	Learn from your past failures, but don't let these define your future. Instead, see them as a lesson for future success.
086	Train your discomfort muscle with small challenges and avoid the panic mode.
087	Learn to access your reserve tank by not giving up the first and second time. You have always 60 percent left, the first time you think you are done.
088	If you don't know that you procrastinate, it will be hard to fight it. Use the 30 signs that you are a Procrastinator to become more aware of your procrastination temptation.
089	Use one of your temptations, like watching a particular TV series, as a starting engine for a must-do activity. jCom both activities together. Only if you start the must-do activity, you are allowed to do your temptation activity as well. And as soon as you stop your must-do activity, you stop the other as well.
090	Seek an Accountabilabuddy to support you to follow through on your goals and to be more accountable.
091	Use Results-thinking to help you see the big picture and estimate early if your goal is feasible and what it takes to achieve your goal. Otherwise, you will increase the chance of failure and procrastination.

Nr.	Anti-Procrastination Hack
092	Don't let your frustrations and disappointments make you procrastinate or give-up entirely. Instead, see them as a signal that you need to use your Process-thinking more or better. Challenge yourself to develop your Process-thinking skills.
093	Hard Work times Many equals Result. To know which hard work you need to do, you need both Results-thinking and Process-thinking. To actually perform the hard work, you need Process-thinking.
094	Be aware of the Stockdale Paradox and find the right balance between focusing on your end goal and focusing on the process goals for today.
095	To stop procrastinating and become successful in pursuing your goals, you need both Results-thinking as well as Process-thinking. But you need to balance both in the right way.
096	Every result is a consequence of a series of actions. Process-thinking means that you are aware that you can only change your result by changing your actions. Track down the actions which need to be improved and start improving them.
097	You don't change your results with Results-thinking. Instead, you need to stop with Results-thinking and start with Process-thinking if you want to get better results.

Nr.	Anti-Procrastination Hack
098	Once per day, evaluate how you have balanced your Process-thinking with Results-thinking. Evaluate based on what went well and what went wrong that day and take new decisions for the next day.
099	To be able to do Process-thinking, create a list of next steps you need to take for the upcoming days, for each of your goals.
100	To start with Process-thinking or Results-thinking, use the two-step process. First, define the scope of your thinking, then ask yourself the different questions within the chosen scope.
101	Schedule a daily meeting with yourself where you think strategically about the way you use Process-thinking and Results-thinking effectively and how you can improve on that.
102	Use Negative Visualization to reduce your fear of failure, fear of success, and fear of the unknown. Practicing Negative Visualization will boost your confidence, productivity, success, and happiness.
103	Protect yourself from being blinded by the tip of the iceberg by realizing that there is a law of nature that says that behind every success an incredibly large and complex world is hidden that you don't see.
104	Let your future-self motivate you to perform the tasks you have to do. Just visualize your future-self and how he will feel about doing or not doing the task.

Nr.	Anti-Procrastination Hack
105	Check with your future-self whether or not your goals are appropriate for you to work on or not.
106	Give your daily actions a bigger purpose to help you motivate to do the tasks you need to do and become a goal getter.
107	Deal with setbacks upfront adequately so that they don't stand between you and your goal. Use future-self visualization to develop counter scenarios for future setbacks.
108	Strengthen your Anti-Procrastination Mindset and become a highly productive goal getter by visualizing your future-self regularly and seeing your potential to grow and develop yourself.
109	Alternate your associated state of awareness with a dissociated state of awareness when doing future-self visualization. This will motivate you to do the work and will kill your procrastination.
110	Use future-self visualization to perform an ecology check on your goals to make sure that you are working on the right goals and that they don't conflict with your other goals or the people around you. Only then you will be sure that your goal is feasible and that you have the chance to see it through until it is complete.
111	Use "I am ..." statements to stop yourself from procrastinating so that you will tap into the power of your identity. Combine your "I am ..." statements with future-self visualization.

Nr.	Anti-Procrastination Hack
112	Make sure that the communication between your conscious and subconscious mind is optimal by bringing your mind in a relaxed state.
113	Make future-self visualization a daily habit, so your priorities will always be on top of your mind.
114	Make your visualization as rich as possible and incorporate all your senses. This activates and engages your whole brain.
115	Follow the three rules for crafting exciting, compelling and motivating positive affirmations which have the power to help you get your stuff done and finally achieve some results.
116	Use Positive Affirmations to beat your procrastination temptation and to take control of your subconscious mind.
117	Watch your language and choose your words wisely when you talk to yourself. The most effective way to communicate with yourself is to give yourself very precise instructions so that exactly the right neural networks in your brain are fired off without costing it you too much mental energy. If you want to achieve something, help yourself by stating it in the present tense and in a positive way.
118	Start to see making mistakes as a way to quickly discover the dead-end signs on your way to your goal. The quicker you know that you are on a dead-end, the quicker you will find your way to your goal. So, start making mistakes as quickly as possible because it will make you more successful in achieving your goals!

The Anti-Procrastination Mindset

Private VIP Facebook Group

As we have seen in this book, procrastination is something you can easily overcome by implementing small anti-procrastination hacks one at a time. The real secret to changing your mindset into an Anti-Procrastination Mindset is continuous development. Furthermore, we have seen that having an Accountabilabuddy can be of great help. But where do you find your Accountabiliabuddy? What if you would have not one but many Accountabilabuddies?

Well, I have good news for you! I have created a Special VIP Facebook Group for you to join. And the good news is, it's FREE!

Together we can help each other held accountable for implementing the anti-procrastination hacks.

If you would like to be a member, for FREE, of this community

If you follow this QR code with a QR reader on your smartphone, then you will arive on the Facebook group. Just click JOIN and you're good to go:

Until we meet in our Private VIP Facebook Group,

Live Fully, Be Awesome!

Cheers, Harry

One more thing ...

Enjoy this book?

You can make a big difference!

Getting feedback is very important for everyone. So, also for me! If you enjoyed reading this book and found it useful, would you do me a favor, of leaving me an honest review on Amazon? That would mean a lot to me!

Your support really does make a big difference, both for me as for other readers. I read all the reviews personally, so I can get your feedback and make this book even better.

Reviews are one of the most powerful tools in my arsenal when it comes to getting attention for my books. Much as I would like to, I don't have the financial muscle of a New York publisher. I can't take out full-page ads in the newspaper or put posters on the subway. But I do have something much more powerful and effective than that: it's YOU! And that is something that those publishers would kill to get their hands on.

Honest reviews of my books will help to bring my books to the attention of other readers. If you've enjoyed this book, I would be very grateful if you could spend just five minutes leaving a review (it can be as short as you like) on the Amazon review page for this book.

If you just follow this QR code with the QR app on your smartphone, then you immediately land on the book review page for this book on Amazon:

Just scroll down to the Customer reviews section and click the yellow button which says "Write a customer review."

Customer reviews

There are no customer reviews yet.

5 star		0%
4 star		0%
3 star		0%
2 star		0%
1 star		0%

Share your thoughts with other customers

Write a customer review

Thanks again for your support! it means the world to me!!

And until we meet in our private VIP Facebook Group,

Live Fully, Be Awesome!

Cheers, Harry

About the Author

Harry Heijligers is the founder of Smart Leadership Hut; an online place for managers and leaders to brush up their Smart Leadership skills and continuously work on improving their stakeholder influence.

Harry has been a project manager for over 25 years and has accomplished various projects in Business and IT and most of the time on the intersection of both: organizational restructuring, introducing and implementing new service models, replacing large CRM and BSS systems, Lean Six Sigma projects and so on.

The common denominator in all projects I did, was change and how to deal with resistance to change within all stakeholders. That's why Harry also searched for tools to develop his stakeholder influence because this is not something which is being taught in school, right?

So, in 1998, Harry started his path in becoming an expert in NLP and all kinds of other social skills, resulting in becoming an international certified NLP trainer in 1999.

Since then, Harry has trained dozens of project managers in the Netherlands, where he lives, in life training seminars. While Harry wanted to expand his reach to other project managers in the world, he decided to start Smart Leadership Hut, where he will train all principles needed to gain more influence over your stakeholders via online training courses. Harry loves educating and inspiring managers and leaders to succeed and live the life of their dreams.

Furthermore, Harry is an author and blogger. He has a Dutch blog on HarryHeijligers.com, and he is blogging for SmartLeadershipHut.com.

Harry lives in Maastricht in The Netherlands with his wife and two kids.

More Books by Harry Heijligers

How the world of Wow begins Now! – A beginners Guide to the Internet of Things

Printed in Great Britain
by Amazon